Father Knows Less

G. P. Putnam's Sons
New York

Father Knows Less

· or ·

"Can I Cook My Sister?"

. . .

One Dad's Quest to Answer
His Son's Most Baffling Questions

. . .

Wendell Jamieson

G. P. PUTNAM'S SONS
Publishers Since 1838
Published by the Penguin Group
Penguin Group (USA) Inc., 375 Hudson Street, New York, New York 10014, USA • Penguin Group (Canada), 90 Eglinton Avenue East, Suite 700, Toronto, Ontario M4P 2Y3, Canada (a division of Pearson Penguin Canada Inc.) • Penguin Books Ltd, 80 Strand, London WC2R 0RL, England • Penguin Ireland, 25 St Stephen's Green, Dublin 2, Ireland (a division of Penguin Books Ltd) • Penguin Group (Australia), 250 Camberwell Road, Camberwell, Victoria 3124, Australia (a division of Pearson Australia Group Pty Ltd) • Penguin Books India Pvt Ltd, 11 Community Centre, Panchsheel Park, New Delhi–110 017, India • Penguin Group (NZ), 67 Apollo Drive, Rosedale, North Shore 0745, Auckland, New Zealand (a division of Pearson New Zealand Ltd) • Penguin Books (South Africa) (Pty) Ltd, 24 Sturdee Avenue, Rosebank, Johannesburg 2196, South Africa

Penguin Books Ltd, Registered Offices:
80 Strand, London WC2R 0RL, England

Published simultaneously in Canada

Library of Congress Cataloging-in-Publication Data

Jamieson, Wendell.
Father knows less, or, "Can I cook my sister?" : one dad's quest to answer his son's most baffling questions / Wendell Jamieson.
p. cm.
ISBN 978-0-399-15442-3
1. Children's questions and answers. 2. Child rearing. I. Title. II. Title: Father knows less. III. Title: "Can I cook my sister?"
HQ784.Q4J36 2007 2007023054
306.874'2—dc22

Printed in the United States of America
1 3 5 7 9 10 8 6 4 2

BOOK DESIGN BY AMANDA DEWEY
ILLUSTRATIONS BY MEIGHAN CAVANAUGH

For Helene

Father Knows Less

1.

Why?

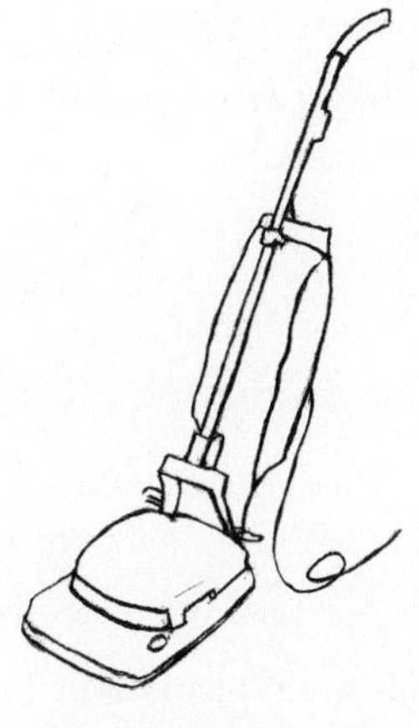

I remember the white-hot highway, the exploding chrome highlights of the other cars, the blast of humid air through the open windows. But most of all, I remember the roar of the road.

Our blue Volkswagen station wagon had no air conditioner. The engine was in the back, not under the hood, so it vibrated and heated up the rear seats where my sister and I sat, lap belts loose around our waists. We didn't have much to do back there—this was before Walkmans or iPods or portable DVD players, and the whipping wind violently fanned the pages of any book we tried to open—so we just sautéed in silent misery. Outside, Long Island flew by like a freight train, the summer sun burning away all the textures of the world and turning each receding line of trees and houses a lighter shade of green-gray.

I must have been five. With nothing else to do, I began to daydream.

This can be dangerous.

I didn't think about our destination, the little brown house on stilts we rented near the beach on Dune Road. Nor did I look forward to playing in the sand, or in the bay, or watching the sailboats glide beneath the drawbridges that connected Dune Road with the mainland. And I didn't ruminate on the horseshoe crabs I'd see crawling along the silt, even though, unchanged for hundreds of millions of years, they are among the most bizarre and fascinating creatures on earth.

I thought about something else.

Why was the road so incredibly noisy? Where was the sound coming from? How can wind make noise? It's just air, invisible air, moving fast, right? And in this case, the air wasn't even moving—the car was. So why was the highway so loud?

I leaned forward and shouted to my father. I may have had to do this a few times to be heard.

"Daddy, why is the highway so loud?"

Here is what he said:

"Because all the people who live next to the road have their vacuum cleaners on."

I knew vacuums were noisy; I thought of ours at home, thundering along the rug. Then I imagined one blasting away in every other house and made some careful sonic calculations in my head. His answer made perfect sense. I leaned back, satisfied, returning to my spot in the wind tunnel.

Cut to Christmas morning, a few years later:

We lived in a brownstone row house in a neighborhood in Brooklyn called Park Slope. We always had very nice Christmases here, both before my parents got divorced and after. My sister, Lindsay, and I would get up in the milky early-morning light, retrieve our bulging stockings from the mantelpiece and spill them out on our beds. We'd tally everything up. Then we'd get our parents through the glass-paneled doors that separated our rooms and drag them, groggy but game, downstairs to the tree.

But this year was different. Lindsay had lost a tooth on Christmas Eve and placed it beneath her pillow. The first thing she did when she got up was look to see if the tooth was still there, even before retrieving her stocking. And it was.

"Daddy," she called, bursting angrily through those glass-paneled doors, her feet stomping. "Daddy, wake up. The tooth fairy didn't come. My tooth is still there. There's no money under my pillow. Why didn't the tooth fairy come?"

Here is what he said:

"She got run over by Santa Claus's sleigh."

My mother laughed. My sister did not.

Children ask questions; that's a fact. For someone whose age is in the low to mid single digits, the world is a blank slate waiting to be asked about, every long-held assumption and familiar sight to a tired adult an intriguing and potentially fascinating mystery. And every answer can beget a new question, until parent and child are locked in that final single-word checkmate: "Why?"

Every parent, I imagine, has his or her own technique for dealing with this phenomenon. Some improvise, some turn to the dictionary, some go online, some say, "Ask your father," or "Ask your mother." Some just shrug and say, "I don't know"—a phrase that would seem like a surefire way to end the process but can be surprisingly ineffective. My father, on the road or in the bed on Christmas morning, liked to make things up. This wasn't necessarily because he didn't know the answers, or that he found the questions annoying, or that he was drunk. It just seemed to amuse him, giving funny answers. My mother laughed along, too—hey, Wendell, you didn't really think everyone by the side of the road had a vacuum on, did you?

I was twenty-two, driving down the Long Island Expressway in my own un-air-conditioned Volkswagen, when suddenly it hit me: I'd been duped.

Of course, my father didn't always make stuff up. Sometimes he thoughtfully tried to explain the world, even when it was scary.

I was watching the news one evening in the living room. I did this every night: even today I can recall the twin sensations—audio and tactile—of hearing Walter Cronkite's voice (*"And that's the way it is . . ."*) while wearing footie pajamas. My cousins from North Carolina used to say I was a weirdo, always watching the news, but I was entranced. On this particular evening, with my parents entertaining neighbors in the kitchen, the stories and pictures were especially fascinating: war in the Middle East. A very pale-looking man, speaking slowly and with apparent pain, appeared on the screen. He described being tortured. He said electrodes had been attached to his testicles.

"Daddy," I screamed. "WHAT ARE TESTICLES?"

My father came in from the kitchen. He leaned down, lowered his voice and said, "Testicles are the little things underneath your penis."

I was horrified. Why would anyone do *that* to another person?

I wished he'd made something up.

Now I have two children of my own. The older one, Dean, is seven and has been in full-bore question mode for about four years. It began as a trickle, turned into a rushing stream and then a wild river. Why do ships have round windows? What does it feel like to get stabbed? Are killer whales mean? Am I allergic to metal? Can a crow peck your eyes out? Why do you like beer? Why can't I drink beer? Why were the Nazis bad? What's a cadaver? Why do policemen like doughnuts? Why, why, why, WHY?

I've wondered how to handle this. What do I do with the questions that I cannot answer, and those I'd like to know the answer to myself? (Why, exactly, *do* policemen like doughnuts?) Do I reveal to Dean that I am but a mere mortal? I think of my dad and the roadside vacuum cleaner symphony. I wouldn't want Dean going through life believing something like that. Well, it would be funny, but . . .

My cousins from North Carolina like to talk about me watching Walter Cronkite because I eventually became a newspaper reporter and editor. Maybe the two are related; perhaps that's where it started. Or maybe it started with the rolled-up copy of *The New York Times* that appeared inside the front gate of the house in Park Slope each morning, freezing to the touch and dusted with snow in January, limp from humidity in August. Either way, as I think about Dean and his questions, the irony is clear: I ask questions for a living, whether interviewing the mayor or a policeman or a grieving widow, or asking a reporter who has just come into the newsroom what the mayor or policeman or grieving widow had to say. I met my wife, Helene, at a newspaper: she was a crime reporter; I wrote obituaries. (*"What's a cadaver?"*) We courted with questions. For us, with our tiny first-newspaper salaries, questions were sometimes the only commodity we had to work with.

I ask, and sometimes I get answers.

So I began writing down Dean's questions, no matter how strange or dark or ridiculous. I used pencils and pens and computers, whatever was at hand when the question popped out; once, on the street, I called the office and left myself a voice message. I thought it would be fun to show him all the questions he had asked when he got older. But then I had a better idea.

I'd give him the answers, every last one.

I planned my strategy. Should I open books or cruise the Internet? Too easy. No, I'd really give myself a challenge: I'd get each answer from a real person who knows it by heart, someone whose very livelihood depends on the knowledge that he carries in his head, or someone whose personal experience is an answer in itself. I'd make nothing up, tempting as that might be. I'd call fire chiefs and doctors and paleontologists and movie directors and astronauts and ship captains and magicians and my mother-in-law and anyone else who might know a thing or two about something a seven-year-old wants to know. This would be my gift to him.

But I wouldn't sugarcoat and I wouldn't simplify. If Dean wants the answer, he's going to get it—unedited, unexpurgated, with all its scientific minutiae and detail. I'm taking a stand for all parents who, whether rushing to get out the door in the morning, squinting to see the highway exit sign in the sun, straining to catch the weather report on the radio or craving that first sip of wine after a tough day at the office, must pause for sometimes crucial seconds to explain why blood is warm, why we have eyebrows, why people race cars or why the dollar sign has an S in it. So I'd slake the curiosity of my friends' children, and the children of their friends, too. I'd take questions from boys and girls everywhere, the sons and daughters of friends and strangers, and I'd nail them. Maybe by the time Dean is twenty-two and riding down the highway in his own hot car, he'll understand it all.

My daughter, Paulina, is three and has not yet started to ask about everything. But when I look into her giant brown-black eyes, I know what's going on. They are taking it all in, supplying the raw material for the questions she's storing in the file cabinet inside her head. She is reviewing them, alphabetizing them, collating them, polishing them, preparing them for the day when they will be unleashed in a rushing avalanche, a cascading mountain of queries, to bury her father once and for all, to finish the job her brother began.

Well, little one, bring it on.

I'm ready.

"Why is the highway so loud?"

—WENDELL JAMIESON, age five, in the summer of 1971

Geoffrey Patterson, motion picture sound mixer on dozens of films, including *Twister*, for which he was nominated for an Academy Award:

> "There's the engine, the exhaust pipes, there is aerodynamic resistance—which is the wind noise—there's horns and there are radios. But the number-one cause—seventy-five percent—of all freeway noise is the tires, the friction of the rubber on the asphalt. The solution, ironically enough, is that the more progressive state transportation agencies are using old rubber tires in their asphalt reconstruction projects. The rubberized asphalt reduces the freeway noise by five decibels. To give you an idea, a reduction of ten decibels would be perceived by the human ear as half as loud. So it's kind of a clever solution, using tires to combat the tire noise. When we are making a movie, we have to play the cards that are dealt us, and the only way we can beat it is to hope that actors are louder than the freeway."

"Why do policemen like doughnuts?"

—DEAN JAMIESON

John F. Timoney, Chief of the Miami Police Department, former First Deputy Commissioner, New York City Police Department:

"It's because doughnut stores, especially in New York City, are everywhere, they're ubiquitous, and they are often open twenty-four hours day. The ethnic foods can change from neighborhood to neighborhood, but the one staple is coffee and doughnuts. It's quick and easy; if while you are eating in the car you happen to get an emergency call, you can discard them easily—the loss isn't a hell of a lot. You throw them out the window and you are gone. It's always easy enough to get more."

2.

Weird Science

On my ninth birthday, we shot rockets into the sky.

I built them up in my room, cardboard tubes with balsa wood fins and nose cones. Oblivious to the weather or the time of day, I'd spend hours sanding, gluing and painting, then wetting the decals so they slid easily off the paper sheet on which they'd come—the last step, and a truly delicate art. My concentration was total: I could hear people moving around other parts of the house, could sense the distant presence of my father, mother and sister, and occasionally hear their voices, but that was the only hint that anyone besides me was alive on the planet.

The rockets came in pieces jumbled in loose plastic bags from a company called Estes, which also made the engines—hard battery-sized tubes of potassium nitrate, sulfur and charcoal. My first attempts had been utter failures, the fins out of whack, the decals on diagonally and wrinkled at the edges. But by the time my birthday arrived, with the small leaves outside my window an electric early-spring green, I had become a master. The rockets were balanced, aligned and painted, ready for space travel.

We lived a few blocks from the park, which is where my dad took us on that May Saturday, launchers and rockets in hand. My friends and I, all long hair and bell-bottoms, set up camp at the center of the largest meadow. The sky was a soft spring blue asking to be explored.

The science of these rockets was simple but thrilling: an electrical charge sparked an igniter in a tiny hole at the bottom of the engine, setting off the fuel. With nowhere else to go, the thrust would shoot down, and the rocket would suddenly be a tiny speck trailed by streaming white smoke up, way up, above the trees. An explosive charge would pop off the nose cone at the apex of the rocket's journey, deploying the parachute, and the rocket would come swinging down to earth, not quite floating and not quite falling, and smelling of sulfur.

Those rockets and that birthday occurred at the apex of my space phase, and were the closest my interests ever brought me to science. It was 1975. In retrospect the 1970s do not seem like a hugely scientific decade, and our house was certainly not a hugely scientific place—my father was the vice president of a box-making company owned by his father, and my mother, having stayed home after my sister and I were born, was beginning a career as a goldsmith. Yet there was enough going on in the world to draw a little boy's eyes skyward.

I watched the last moon shot on a black-and-white television, and waited breathlessly in summer day camp a few years later as the first images came back from the Viking probe showing the red and rock-strewn surface of Mars. Anything about the search for life in distant galaxies fascinated me; I was frustrated that the Viking could not answer, unequivocally, the question of whether there had been life on that planet. For every mystery solved in those days, there seemed to be a million new questions.

Science is the beginning of all questions. Even when it cannot take the mysteries of the world, conquer them and put them in a safe place, at the very least it can lay out questions of spectacular wonderment and illustrate them. And science holds endless fascination for a child. On the great list of all the questions asked by all the children in all the world, science surely earns the highest tally.

"How far up can my balloon go before it pops?"

"If Jupiter is made out of gas, can it make our car go?"

"Why is the sky blue?"

I wasn't expecting to find life in distant galaxies with my little rockets, but I was trying to make my contribution to the space race. The tallest one I had, about three feet, had multiple stages—the charge at the top of one engine would ignite the one above it. Simple, but identical in theory to the multiple stages of Apollo 17, the final moon shot, whose thundering nighttime launch I had watched before bedtime.

Those Estes rockets made me wonder about the world. How far up could I shoot them? What modifications could I make to get them to go higher, to stay aloft longer? And what was the view like up there—could you see over the rooftops of our neighborhood all the way to the skyscrapers of Manhattan?

We took turns pressing the launch button, creating an unseen electrical circuit that sparked the igniters. One by one the rockets shot skyward with a *phffffffffffffffffffft*, and one by one we went running after them, bell-bottoms flapping. My dad seemed to get a kick out of the whole thing, carefully monitoring the launch procedures and clapping with an especially good shot.

And he groaned with us at the occasional failure: the rocket that got stuck on the launch pad, and then deployed its own parachute, pathetically, while still sitting on the ground.

But there were only a few misfires; most lifted off as planned. If we were lucky, a rocket would land back in the grassy meadow near us. If we were unlucky, it would drift into the nearby trees, its parachute snagged on a branch. If we were really unlucky, it would float into a group of teenagers nearby who would either keep it, break it or demand money for its return.

We stayed lucky and just a little unlucky and soon a group of kids and adults of different ages and colors had gathered around to watch. *Phffffffffffffffffffft* went the rockets. Everyone asked questions about what we were doing, how it all worked. The little rockets hung up in the pale blue sky. A couple of guys with long hair and jean shorts stood on the periphery and seemed the most awestruck by each successive launch, loudly exclaiming how much it amazed them. In time I've come to realize that of course they had been completely stoned.

Eventually, two police officers (they had long hair, too) came over, watched for a minute and then took my dad aside. He came back, looking annoyed, and started packing everything up. "Come on, kids," he said. "Let's go back to the house for cake."

Now that I'm a parent, I try my best to embrace and encourage any scientific interest Dean has. But getting him excited has been a challenge: he's not quite old enough for rockets yet. His school does a good job with the basics, on reading and writing and math, but the science curriculum is limited. Stories about this pop up from time to time in the newspaper. Advocacy groups release reports or hold press conferences to complain and raise alarm bells about the school system's inability to produce the scientists of the future.

So Helene and I have signed Dean up for extra science classes after school. When I get home from work, I ask him what he's learned. Usually he says, "I forget," and goes back to whatever he's doing. But one day he said: "Energy!"

"What do you mean?"

"Look," he said.

He picked up a little rubber cone and squeezed it between his fingers. He squeezed and squeezed, scrunching his face. Then the cone popped out and flew across the room, nearly hitting his sister in the eye. "See?" he said. "Energy."

"That's great, kid."

I pictured hundreds of little boys, rows upon untold rows of them, popping little rubber cones, the energy somehow harnessed and used to power a supertanker across the Pacific Ocean.

Television, usually an ominous and wasteful influence, can actually help when it comes to prompting or strengthening childhood interests. Dean became fascinated by volcanoes and the havoc they can cause because he saw a network broadcast of the movie *Volcano*, starring Tommy Lee Jones and Anne Heche. I shielded his eyes during the scary parts, such as the moment when two firemen are incinerated by a lava flow in downtown Los Angeles.

The film sparked a lengthy and intense volcano phase in our apartment: every conceivable object was categorized by how quickly it would melt/burn/explode when dropped in or consumed by lava. Dean wondered what would happen to an airplane that flew over a volcano. One day when our car was stuck on a muddy road, he gazed out the window and asked, "What would happen if lava went on dirt?"

Helene made a volcano cake for his fifth and sixth birthdays—four ascending layers of decreasing circumference with a hole in the middle in which a red egg mixture, dry ice and warm water were combined, creating a lot of smoke and a sort-of lava flow that made Dean's friends scream and was duly recorded on videotape.

We try to make Dean's birthdays as special as my parents made my ninth. Helene is usually the driving force on this. My contribution to the volcano cake extravaganza was traveling to The Ice House next to an elevated train line in a tough neighborhood to buy the dry ice (solid carbon dioxide). It was a chilly day and the place seemed deserted; the office was empty. Then I rapped on the corrugated metal fence next to the parking lot out back and a large man appeared. He told me dry ice cost $20 for a ten-pound bag.

"But I only need a little piece for a volcano cake," I said.

He gave me a long, hard look. Then he disappeared behind the fence. I stood there stamping my feet to keep warm for at least five minutes—two trains clattered by—before he came back with a small bag. "Two dollars," he said, handing it over. I asked him if there was anything I should know about handling this stuff and he said, "Just don't touch it!" As he walked away, he shook his head back and forth as if he'd never heard anything so insane.

The next year, as "Volcano Cake: The Sequel" was being prepared in the apartment, I returned to The Ice House and this man and I had, word for word, the exact same exchange.

Sometimes Helene takes Dean to the little library near our apartment, even though it is so small it has about eight books and is often closed in winter because of a "lack of heat." The only problem is, there are other children there.

Nothing is worse for a parent than meeting a kid the same age or younger than yours who knows more than your kid does. Knowledge is one of the biggest gifts you can give your child. It gets you ahead in this world, and you hate for anyone to have more of it. As we search for knowledge for our son, we are constantly reminded of the knowledge he, and we, don't possess. If it's other parents telling you how smart their son or daughter is, well, that's okay—they're usually exaggerating, focusing on one area of expertise while ignoring other areas of sub-par knowledge: you can always put their kid under the hot lights until you are satisfied your kid knows something that their kid does not. But when it's the kid talking, well, that can be tough.

The library was empty except for Helene and Dean, who was four, and two little boys who seemed to be about the same age. They were accompanied by one of their mothers. Everyone was sitting at the same table when the boys got into an animated discussion about the solar system. Not only did they know all the planets by name, size and defining characteristic, but they were able to categorize which were the outer planets and which were the inner planets. Dean had no idea what they were talking about. I doubt he even knew the name of the planet he was standing on.

Helene confronted me about this when I got home. I didn't even have time to take my coat off.

"We have to start working on Dean," she began. "There were these kids at the library, they were four, two boys, and they knew everything about the planets, so much more than him. They knew which were the outer planets and which were the inner planets." Her voice reached a high pitch. "We're not teaching him enough!"

"Dean knows the planets," I said. I'm not sure why I said this.

"No he doesn't."

"Yes he does."

"Okay," Helene said. "Ask him."

Dean was nearby, playing with a truck. I knelt down.

"Hey, Dino, do you know the planets?"

"No."

"Oh, come on. Yes you do. We've talked about them. You can name them. Let's start with the first one, the one near the sun."

I waited.

"You know, the little orange one?"

I waited.

"It starts with M?"

He looked at me.

"Eminy?" he said.

So began a brief but very, very intense planet-education phase in our apartment. The next day Helene bought a large collection of small and large Styrofoam balls—I have no idea where she found them—fishing line, paper clips, paint and plastic hooks, as well as a bag of glow-in-the-dark star stickers. She and Dean spent the afternoon painting the balls, using her college astronomy textbook as a guide, and when I got home I was instructed to go down to the basement to get the ladder.

Then I was up near the ceiling in Dean's room, gluing the hooks in place and attaching fishing line to each. I stuck half-straightened paper clips into the crunchy planets and started tying them to the lines. I flashed back to those little rockets shooting into the sky above Prospect Park before the police came and shut down the party. I had no trouble with Mercury (Eminy), Venus, Earth, Mars, Jupiter and Saturn, but started to get a little hazy as I reached the outer planets.

Let me tell you this: while it is painful to encounter a four-year-old who knows more than your four-year-old does, it is even more painful to encounter a four-year-old who knows more than you do.

"Hey, honey, which is next, Uranus or Neptune?"

Helene came into the room and looked up at me. She crinkled her forehead. "You know, I'm not sure. I don't remember. I think . . . Wait, let me get the book."

I balanced on the ladder while she ran into the living room. She came back and started flipping through the dog-eared pages. "Here, it is. Um, Neptune comes first. No, no—it's Uranus."

That was easy. But then another question presented itself. As I prepared to hang Pluto and move on to the stars, a vague recollection came to me: Hadn't I recently read a story, or seen on the news, that Pluto actually was not a planet? I called Helene back. "Honey, wasn't Pluto, like, thrown out of the planets?"

She remembered it, too, sort of. Her textbook, however, predated the question by several decades.

So she went on the Internet. I came down, had a beer and watched some television. The ladder waited. She spent an hour doing research.

Here's what she found:

The question of whether Pluto was a planet or not was the rage of the astronomical world. Thought to be a mixture mostly of rock, nitrogen and methane ice (*"Just don't touch it!"*), the distant sphere Helene and I had grown up with was now classified by many as a plutino, and while it retained its status as the ninth member of our solar system at most major observatories and planetariums, the Rose Science Center at the American Museum of Natural History had, indeed, thrown it out of the planets.

Pluto had a lot going against it: smaller than our moon—only 1,440 miles in diameter—it travels through space as part of the Kuiper Belt of asteroids. That fact violates one of the new defining characteristics of a planet, Helene learned: its orbit must be cleared of all other objects. We considered our options. Then I pointed out that we already had the little blue ball of Styrofoam, it already had a straightened paper clip in it and it already had a hook on the ceiling waiting for it.

In our apartment, we decided, Pluto would remain classified as a planet. I went back up the ladder.

Dean was nearby, playing with a truck.

"What happens if your plane flies over a volcano?"

—DEAN

British Airways Captain Eric Moody (retired), who managed to land his Boeing 747 after all four engines died while flying through a cloud of volcanic ash from Mount Galunggung in Java on June 24, 1982:

> "The first thing that we saw was the most wonderful display of a phenomenon known as Saint Elmo's fire. It is an electrical discharge that occurs when something like metal passes through air with a high moisture content, and it manifests itself initially as shimmering lights of all colors; they shimmer up and down the windscreen. As it gets more and more intense, it can develop into short bursts of lightning no more than six to nine inches long, and they dance up and down the windows. As we got farther into this cloud, it developed more into what I imagine tracers would look like coming off the nose; it was sparks. We didn't know what was happening. This was a very dark old night.

"After we'd been watching this for a very short time, the flight engineer noticed that number four engine was running down, or stopping. We shut that engine down properly—we used the classic Boeing engine-closing drill. The other engines stopped almost simultaneously. And then we were the proud possessors of the world's heaviest and largest glider.

"We glided the airplane down from thirty-seven thousand feet to about twelve thousand. It took fourteen minutes. It was a very, very smooth episode, there was nothing violent about it; the plane flew beautifully with the engines down. The passengers knew nothing until the oxygen masks dropped down into the cabin at about eighteen thousand feet. I was thinking quite lucidly, and I asked to reinstate the number four engine because it was the least seriously damaged one. The engineer told me that the manual barred us from restarting an engine that we'd shut down, and I said, 'Oh, bugger the manual.' That was the first one to start up, at thirteen thousand feet, and then a minute and twenty seconds later, number three started up, and twenty or thirty seconds after that the other two started. Then we were back in business.

"I don't think they'll ever know for sure what happened. It has got to be one of three things. It's either the fact that the ash is so dense in the air that it makes the air incompressible, and you need to compress the air in a jet engine; or that the ash was so dense in the air that it expelled all the oxygen and you need oxygen. But more likely it was a combination of both of those, and it was like throwing sand on a barbecue."

"What happens when lava goes on dirt?"

—DEAN

Mark H. Anders, associate professor of earth and environmental sciences, Columbia University, New York City:

"A hot lava will have two effects. One, the heat of the lava will 'bake' the dirt, and two, the dirt will 'freeze' the lava. So geologically we refer to the contact of a lava as a 'baked zone.' The overlying lava often cools quickly, sometimes forming a glass. Often in the case of rhyolites the result is obsidian, or black glass. The dirt will often form a bright red horizon. This may in part be due to fluids—heated by the lava—depositing iron oxides, which are typically bright red or rouge."

"Why is the sky blue?"

—MAXIMO GIOVANNI ROJAS BAUSO, age five, Portland, Oregon

Geza Gyuk, Ph.D., research scientist, director of astronomy at the Adler Planetarium, Chicago:

"At first people thought the sky was blue because there were water droplets in it, but if that were true you'd get a deeper blue when the air is more humid, and that's not the case. After a little more investigation, they realized that the blue was due to the air molecules in the atmosphere. The light from the sun is made up of many different colors; each of those colors is a different wavelength of light. The wavelength of red, for example, is longer than the wavelength of blue. Longer wavelengths, for the most part, travel straight through air molecules, while shorter ones are more scattered by them. So when the blue wavelengths hit the air molecules, they are scattered all over the sky—and that's what you see when you look up. This is called Rayleigh Scattering and was discovered by Lord Rayleigh. (Many of the early physicists were either sirs or lords because they were the only ones with time on their hands.) Red wavelengths can also scatter, of course. At sunset, when the sun is lower on the horizon, the light from it must travel through many more air molecules than when it is right above us. All these molecules scatter the red wavelengths, too, and that's why the sun looks red at the end of the day."

"If a black hole sucks in everything, why doesn't it suck in the black part of the hole?"

—NATE CONRAD, age five, Rockaway, New Jersey

W. Scott Kardel, astronomer, Palomar Observatory, Palomar Mountain, California:

"A black hole is a collapsed region of space with an intense gravitational field. The pull of gravity is so strong that nothing can escape it.

"Think about conditions here on Earth. For a rocket to escape Earth and not fall down, it must travel faster than 25,000 miles per hour (7 miles per second). This is called escape velocity. Anything traveling at a speed less than that will be pulled back down by Earth's gravity. Black holes have a much greater gravitational pull than that of Earth, and as such their escape velocities are much higher. What makes a black hole so unique is that it has an escape velocity that is greater than the speed of light—186,282 miles per second.

"A black hole's darkness isn't an actual thing. Rather it is the absence of a thing—namely light. While matter and energy can be pulled into a black hole, because darkness itself isn't a thing, it cannot be sucked into the black hole."

"If you don't hit anything with it, how does a whip make that noise?"

—GENEVIEVE BOUCHONVILLE, age four, Branchburg, New Jersey

Mistress Jennifer Hunter, a dominatrix, who runs Jennifer Hunter's Ivy League Educated Mistresses:

"That very satisfying and dismaying crack is actually a miniature version of a sonic boom as the very tip of the whip—which is called the 'cracker' or the 'popper' and is actually a tuft of thread or string or nylon—moves faster than the speed of sound and actually breaks the sound barrier. The speed of sound in air is 760 miles per hour—which is Mach 1—so the very tip of the whip is actually going faster than Mach 1. Only whips with crackers or poppers make that sound. The whip is probably the first man-made object to actually break the sound barrier."

ME: *"Do you use a whip on, like, a lot of your clients?"*

"My service is a telephone service."

"Oh. So would you use a whip so your clients can hear you use it on the phone?"

"I would. I would use the whip on the phone because some people love to hear the whip. I was talking to a client and I started whipping a chair and pulled a muscle in my back and was out of commission at the gym for three weeks. I always tell women who work for me, if they don't have a whip, that they can duplicate the whip crack by quickly clapping together blocks of wood."

"What kind of whip do you use?"

"I will often use a dogsled whip. It is actually very beautiful. It is just a black whip, and it is used to control a team of dogs. It is perfect because it is not too long and it is thick enough so that it will sound ominous if it needs to sound ominous. I wouldn't want to go out on the patio and be dealing with a really long whip or a bullwhip because it would put my shoulders right out of commission."

"If Jupiter is made of gas, do we have to drive all the way there to fill our car up?"

—THEO RUSSELL, age three, Brooklyn, New York

Neil deGrasse Tyson, astrophysicist at the American Museum of Natural History, New York City:

"Jupiter is indeed made of gas, but unfortunately, not the kind we would want to put in our cars. The word 'gas' that we find in 'gas station' is short for gasoline, just as 'phone' is short for telephone, and, of course, 'Theo' is short for Theodore. Gasoline is an energy-packed liquid that your car's engine uses to get you from one place to another. The gas on Jupiter is real gas, like the air you breathe, except

Jupiter's gas is made of mostly hydrogen and helium. By the way, if you combine hydrogen and oxygen, you get rocket fuel. So not cars, but spaceships of the future may stop at Jupiter one day to refill their rockets."

"How far up can my balloon go before it pops?"

—ELLIOT APPLEBAUM, age six, La Jolla, California

Donald R. Pettit, astronaut, who spent five and a half months orbiting the Earth as the science officer on the International Space Station:

"First off, it depends on what kind of a balloon—we have Mylar birthday balloons and we have the classic rubber birthday balloon, and the physics will be completely different. The Mylar balloon will have a constant volume as it goes up in the atmosphere because it is a rigid structure. The rubber balloon expands.

"Take a Mylar balloon .8 meters in diameter. Its volume is a quarter of a cubic meter. You fill that with helium. Its density is going to be constant—it weighs what it weighs, its mass stays the same. Let's make a guesstimate of 50 grams of helium, and the balloon weighs about 25 grams, and it's got a volume of a quarter of a cubic meter, so now its density is fixed at 300 grams per cubic meter. At 13,500 meters—44,000 feet—the balloon would stop rising because the density outside is now equal to the density of the balloon. What would probably happen is it would stay up there for a few days, the helium would diffuse through the Mylar and it would slowly deflate, and it would start to come down. The Mylar balloon would have about 10 psi pressure across it and it could also rupture at a seam.

"For the rubber balloon, I'm assuming zero-point-eight meters in diameter, a quarter of a cubic meter when filled, and it's filled with helium. I'm assuming it has the same mass as our Mylar balloon, so it has the same density, 300 grams per cubic meter. Since this is a zero-pressure balloon, made out of rubber, it will expand in proportion to the decrease in atmospheric pressure. In concept, it could go up to real high altitudes; however, you are going to reach the structural limit of the rubber that makes the balloon and it is going to pop. I did a little research and I'm thinking the rubber balloon will probably pop at around 28,000 feet due to the rubber getting brittle from the −40° Celsius temperatures and then rupturing as it tries to further expand. The highest you'll find a commercial airliner, just to compare, is about 40,000 feet."

"Why are planets round?"

—EVA LAFORGE, age five, New York City

Preethi Pratap, Ph.D., astronomer, MIT Haystack Observatory, Westford, Massachusetts:

"Planets are round because gravity pulls them together. Gravity exerts its force equally in all directions, so planets form a naturally round shape. But you have to have enough mass to have gravity. For example, asteroids are not round, they are all kinds of weird shapes. That's because they are not big enough: they don't have enough mass, and hence they don't have enough gravity to pull it into that round shape. The three definitions of a planet are that it is round, that it orbits the sun and that it has cleared all things in its vicinity, that it has a clear orbit."

"Why do things look bigger when I get closer and smaller when I'm far away?"

—LUNA GINSBERG, age three, Austin, Texas

Joel Meyerowitz, award-winning photographer whose work has appeared in more than 350 exhibitions around the world, and whose books include *Cape Light* and *Aftermath: The World Trade Center Archive*:

"When an object—your hand, your mother's face or something big like an ocean liner—is close to your eye it appears to be big because it fills your vision, or what you could call your visual field. As your mother, who has just kissed you good night, stands up and walks out of the room, her face and then her body seem to get smaller and smaller.

"There are two ways to understand this. The first is the physical reality of the object. Your mother's face is ten inches high, and when her face and yours are next to each other you get the full impact of a ten-inch face; when she stands up and is three feet away from you, you can now see her face and half her body, and when she stands in the doorway you see a small face on a tall body. Her face is still ten inches high and if you went over to her with a ruler you would see that is true.

"Then there is something called the 'angular diameter,' which is a way of measuring something from a fixed point (you in bed). As the object you are looking at moves further away, the angular diameter gets smaller. Do an experiment: put a soccer ball, or a book, or any object you like on a shelf and tape a piece of string on top and on the bottom, then bring the two equal pieces of string to a point in the middle of the room. Now you can see, and this is the second way to understand this problem, how the rays of light coming from the top and bottom of the ball are reaching your eye. Can you see how the space between the strings gets bigger as you get closer to the ball? That's the angular diameter. Measure it at one-foot intervals and you will understand why things look smaller when they are further away."

When we are small, The Future holds considerable interest; little do we know how much bill-paying and commuting is involved. The very word suggests cars that fly, and colonies on the Moon, and a world without war or sickness—that, or a barren wasteland depopulated by plague or obliterated by thermonuclear weapons. Either way, it's pretty interesting.

Questions about The Future are hard to answer with any accuracy. Who really knows what's going to happen? At best, they are guesses. But one kind of question about the future can indeed be answered with some certainty: questions that were asked by children years ago.

Lisa and Bill are friends of ours; Bill and I worked together at my last newspaper. Lisa's first husband, Philippe, was French. They had a son, Noel. Lisa wanted to name him Cassady, after Neal Cassady from Jack Kerouac's *On the Road*, but Philippe said *"Non!"* to that—he disliked all things American and didn't speak English.

Noel grew up in northern California; they moved there because Philippe, a street artist who made jewelry from horseshoe nails, thought business might be good in San Francisco. For whatever reason, and there seemed to be several likely ones, the marriage didn't work out. Lisa and Philippe split, and Lisa raised Noel on her own. They moved around a lot as she went from a tiny newspaper to a small newspaper to a medium-sized newspaper, and she worried that all this moving around was taking a toll on her son; that, and the absence of his non-English-speaking father.

When Noel was in sixth grade, he and Lisa lived in Freestone, on the Bohemian Highway, and he attended The Harmony School in Occidental. This was 1986. "It was the greatest address I ever had," Lisa said.

For a class project, Noel had to write his autobiography and put it in a little book with drawings. Lisa, who kept everything her son ever wrote or drew or made, flipped through it not too long ago and found a section marked "Futuristic Questions."

Will cats ever get extinct?

I wonder if people will start installing escalators in their house?

I wonder if the speed limit will ever be 95?

I wonder if pizza will ever be hazardous?

Twenty years later, the questions, and the singular imagination behind them, gave Lisa real insight into the mind of her eleven-year-old boy, now a father himself. "We were moving a lot," she said. "I was having a really hard time keeping it together, and I think he developed this inner life.

"He was so happy and so content in the book," she said, "and it kind of amazes me that he found so much pleasure even though I thought our life was so stressful."

"Will cats ever get extinct?"

—NOEL AMAND, age eleven, Occidental, California

Ted Daeschler, Ph.D., paleontologist, Academy of Natural Sciences, Philadelphia:

"Yes, because in the long view, everything goes extinct. If we look at the past, we see that evolution has helped animals change with their changing environments; however, there have always been extinctions. Not to freak people out, but judging by past performance, all animals in the form that we know them will go extinct and be replaced by something very similar or totally different; certainly the species that we have in our world today will not be here forever."

"I wonder if people will start installing escalators in their house?"

Tom Saxe, Vice President for Worldwide Engineering, Otis Elevator Corp., East Hartford, Connecticut (the company also makes escalators):

"I don't think it will ever happen. Escalators are expensive to install, they have a lot of moving parts, they need a lot of energy, they make a lot of noise. There are the steps, a handrail that has to move, a large motor with a large gearbox that is used to drive it, the whole support structure, tracks for steps to ride on, a controller that you have to activate to start and stop it. An elevator just has the cabin and a counter weight, typically, and a motor with a pulley on it, so it is a very simple system. You see it much more, people installing elevators in their homes. The escalator is really designed for a lot of people, when you want everything to be somewhat opened so they can see, like in a mall."

"I wonder if the speed limit will ever be 95?"

Ed Fischer, Oregon State traffic engineer (oversees speed limit setting for the state):

"I don't think ninety-five is realistic today; we would need a significant change in vehicles and roadways to make it safe. But if you're optimistic about future possibilities, it is *not* impossible. In very limited and controlled applications it very well may be possible. There have been proposals for eighty-mile-per-hour limits in Arizona; and it wasn't too many years ago that Montana proposed no speed limits at all in certain cases. I can imagine a futuristic application of vehicle control technologies on roadways that have been designed for one-hundred-mile-per-hour speeds where a very high speed limit might be possible. However, given the limitations of our highways, our vehicles and our drivers, I believe that the only places we could have speed limits greater than the design speed (usually seventy miles per hour for most rural interstate highways) would be on very long, flat and straight sections of interstate highway without a lot of traffic."

"I wonder if pizza will ever be hazardous?"

Tony Muia, founder of A Slice of Brooklyn Pizza Tour, Brooklyn, New York:

"Pizza is actually good for you. Take the tomato sauce. Lycopene, which occurs naturally in tomatoes, is an anti-carcinogen. Studies have shown that intake of tomatoes and tomato-based products is related to elevated blood lycopene levels and a lower risk of a variety of cancers. As for the mozzarella, how bad can it be? It's got your milk, it's got your protein. Sounds good to me. And as for the crust, you got your wheat, your gluten. Still sounds good to me. You could probably go with a whole wheat crust, which would actually be a bit healthier, but then I don't think that's real pizza.

"Now don't get me wrong, pizza has *not* been healthy for some people. In 1989, in St. Louis, a Domino's pizza delivery driver ran a red light and struck a car driven by forty-nine-year-old Jean Kinder, who suffered injuries to her head and spine. That's when Domino's did away with its delivery-in-thirty-minutes-or-you-receive-the-pie-for-free policy. In the early nineties, at Original Pizza in Brooklyn, three men got into an argument with a pizza maker. They blinded him by throwing flour in his face, then shot him in the head. The pizza maker fought back with a wooden pizza paddle, but was pronounced dead at the scene.

"Then there's Lucchese mobster Ralph (Raffie) Cuomo, who founded the original Ray's Pizza in New York City in 1959 and went to prison for using his landmark Prince Street pizzeria to sell heroin along with pies. He and about thirty others were part of the 'Pizza Connection case,' in which the men were charged with running a heroin ring from several pizza shops. But you didn't hear that from me. As we like to say in Brooklyn, there are three secrets to living a long, healthy life: you don't see nothin', you don't hear nothin' and you don't know nothin'!"

3.

That's Gotta Hurt

Warm blood, watery eyeballs, icky substances that come out of their noses and ears: children are obsessed with their bodies, their first true possessions. They wonder what's beneath their skin, and why their skin is the color it is. They are especially intrigued by the changes that take place for mysterious reasons, like wrinkles that develop in water, and why they have items growing on their bodies that don't seem to have any immediate value, like the hair on their head or above their eyes. Their bodies are a great bottomless well of questions.

They are also entranced by the concept of pain—experiencing it, causing it, understanding it, watching someone else suffer from it. All the objects of the world are lined up in their heads in the order of how much pain they would cause if thrown from a truck or dropped from a cliff. The body is a target waiting to be carved up, flattened or smashed. You are asked to recount various painful episodes of your life, especially those that left scars:

"Did it hurt when the doctor took out your . . . what was it?"

"My appendix."

"Yes, did it hurt?"

"Well, I was asleep."

"Whew. That's lucky."

Pain need not be fatal to be engaging to a child: while it has got to hurt to be consumed by lava, or attacked by a shark—which, we have learned in our nighttime reading, tends to take only one bite out of you before swimming away—minor pain like the burning of eyes by shampoo or the stinging of a bee also fascinates, at least after the screaming has stopped. Dean may be a sophisticated child of the millennium, but he laughs just as hard as his great-grandfather must have when the Three Stooges beat the crap out of each other, even though he claims not to like black-and-white movies.

Look at the paper cut. This phenomenon holds a special place in the hearts of children, and it's easy to understand why: it's truly remarkable that something so flimsy and malleable possesses the power to lash out and make you bleed.

Dean and I were on a train once—we were going to Chicago to see the T-rex named Sue at the Field Museum—when he suddenly put down the book he was looking at. "Daddy—I got a paper cut!" He held his finger up proudly. I leaned close. I squinted. And there, on his finger—I think—was a tiny smudge of red, quite possibly the smallest paper cut in recorded history. Either that or it was a piece of lint.

I wondered if I should pull the emergency brake.

. . .

It makes sense that children are entranced by the concept of pain because they cause an awful lot of it when they get here. Or so I have been told. Helene reminds me of this from time to time. "Childbirth is like being turned inside out," she'll say. I try to imagine this, but all I really have to do is close my eyes and think back to the scene of the crime.

She'd been in labor for nearly three hours that November morning, the sky and the river still dark outside the window. We were in the brand-new obstetrics ward of New York Hospital. Our room had wood paneling and a big television on which the film *Sabrina*, starring William Holden, Humphrey Bogart and Audrey Hepburn, was playing. The nurse and I were trying to enjoy it, but Helene kept interrupting for more ice chips. Also, the wails of women giving birth in other rooms drowned out key bits of dialogue.

I was being careful to remember everything that I saw, everything I heard, because I know children ask about the details of their birth when they are older. I was also born in New York Hospital, in May 1966, just a few years before it became standard for fathers to be let into the delivery room. My mother doesn't remember much about it except the time (10:15 p.m.) and that my father brought her a roast beef sandwich with Russian dressing and a beer after I was born, and it was one of the best things she'd ever tasted.

She also remembers that the night after she was released, while I lay in the nursery beneath fluorescent lights to treat jaundice, she and my father went out to dinner at a restaurant called Le Mistral with his parents. This was a very fancy place in Manhattan that had recently been reviewed in the *Times*. The paper wrote: "This most recent addition to the town's roster of luxury restaurants is a place of estimable charm with a kitchen of considerable merit."

My mother was proud she was able to enjoy Le Mistral so soon after experiencing the physical trauma of having her first child. "I remember that sitting was uncomfortable," she said. I'm oddly proud that my parents were able to enjoy this slice of swanky 1960s New York while their son, me, the most recent addition to the town's roster of screaming infants, baked beneath hot lights a few blocks away.

The intervening thirty-three years had brought quite a few changes to the hospital, not the least of which was the modern ward in which Helene and I now awaited our first child with the television on. Like my mother and father, we didn't know if we were going to have a girl or a boy. Helene had had an epidural, but it had no effect on one mysterious fist-sized "hot spot" on her belly, and she was still very uncomfortable. The nurse implored her to keep pushing as the sky outside lightened and *Sabrina* moved toward its conclusion. The doctor checked in on us from time to time. Finally, after determining that the moment was near, he disappeared for a few nervous-making minutes and came back with a young woman doctor pulling an aluminum cart covered by a sheet of blue paper.

They put on gowns and caps and clear plastic visors, and the woman doctor took the paper off the cart with a flourish worthy of *The Price Is Right.*

On it were two rows of scalpels and scissors, in descending size order, all gleaming in the bright birthing room lights. Helene could not see this, but I could. I leaned in close to her.

I said: "Listen, I don't want to worry you, but you better push as hard as you can."

The young woman doctor said: "Hey—I didn't know William Holden was in this."

Helene said: "Ice chips, more ice chips."

William Holden said: "I was just helping you make up your mind. You ARE in love with her!"

Dean joined us a few minutes later, the scalpels and scissors unused, and then the screaming really began.

It's all well and good and charming when a little baby gets here crying. When he takes his first nap it's a relief—you think, hey, that wasn't so bad. I relaxed as I looked at him sleeping there, black hair coming down over his forehead. He had at least one of my facial characteristics, an oversized upper lip; I gently pressed my little finger into the space between it and his nose and felt the same soft indentation that I'd felt on my own face for thirty-three years, only smaller. His eyes, when open, were giant and an impossibly dark shade of brown. But in my relaxation I was falling into the same trap as the three-year-old who goes to nursery school for the first time and then thinks that that was it, it was only a one-day thing. After forty-eight hours, Helene and I thought we had this parenthood gig in the bag—having a baby seemed easy enough. But on our way home from the hospital, as we drove along the river toward Brooklyn, Dean started screaming again, and it was a deeper, more resonant, more permanent kind of scream.

And it lasted for four months.

In a way, it was his first question, and it was not asked politely. What the hell am I doing in this cold place when I used to be in that nice warm place? Why am I in a big metal box on wheels (our Honda) hurtling down some type of paved corridor (the highway) with other metal boxes on wheels going the same speed in the opposite direction on the other side of a low metal barrier for a cumulative total of a hundred and twenty miles per hour—is this really safe?—with huge geometric shapes on my right (skyscrapers) and a weirdly shimmering and changeable surface on my left (the river)? And what is that other flat surface being held in the air by flimsy-looking strings (the Brooklyn Bridge)?

Helene's mother was at the apartment waiting for us. For the nine years we'd been together, Helene had assured me that if we ever had a baby, her mother would be ready to pitch in and help take care of it, so much so that we'd barely detect a change in our lives. After all, she'd raised three children of her own, and helped out on four other grandchildren so far. Don't worry, Helene said, my mother will take care of everything.

After three days, her mother shrieked: "I've never heard a baby scream like that!" and fled the apartment.

Dean's wails, his unformed questions of alarm, or of pain, prompted our first desperate quest for knowledge as parents. We looked for answers everywhere, beginning with the dozen or so books we'd been given about how to raise children. They all identified the problem as colic, and they all gave different reasons for it and suggested different solutions, usually in an amused tone that was infuriating at 4:30 a.m. We tried over-the-counter medicines, and tea, and putting Dean in his car seat on the dishwasher during the rinse cycle. We rocked him, we rubbed him, we walked the freezing December streets with him. I drove him around in the middle of the night; the screaming stopped only when we went above sixty miles per hour, which is hard to do in Brooklyn (but not impossible).

He screamed through Thanksgiving, he screamed through Christmas. His first pediatrician, Dr. Deutsch, looked at our haggard faces and said, "Oh, just let him cry."

He was fired.

Olga, our fortnightly cleaning lady, suggested in a thick Russian accent that Helene's breast milk was causing the problem. As a visual aid, she pointed to Helene's chest.

She was fired.

Our mailman suggested a liquid remedy with a strange name. It sounded good, and my father, remarkably, found a bottle in a sketchy-looking pharmacy in a sketchy-looking neighborhood. It worked, sort of, but then a friend mentioned that he'd heard this concoction was illegal, and that its magic ingredient was a heavy dose of alcohol.

Stringent postal regulations and intractable union seniority rules, we learned, prevent the firing of one's mailman.

Dean turned yellow, Dean got cradle cap, Dean didn't gain weight as fast as the charts in our parenting books said he should. But most of all, Dean screamed.

I developed Screaming Baby Battle Fatigue. At the newspaper, in my sleep-deprived state, staring vacantly out into the newsroom, someone nearby crinkled plastic wrapping and it sounded like Dean's screams; I nearly jumped out of my seat. Lying awake in bed, I worried that my son, my beautiful two-month-old son, was a rage-a-holic. I imagined my own infant-care product: Baby Sleep-All-Night, complete with a drawing of a blissfully sleeping infant on the cover, a high alcohol content and a dropper in the shape of a bottle of Scotch.

Eventually, we called in reinforcements. With me working nights, and Helene working at home during the days, we had figured we could raise a child without too much outside help besides our parents babysitting from time to time. A few weeks before Dean was born, my mother mentioned that a friend's nanny was free one day a week. We said we weren't interested. A few weeks after he was born, my mother mentioned this again, and we begged for the number.

Brenda was from Nevis and spoke with the gently lilting accent of that island. She came on a Thursday, sat for a brief "interview"—a technicality, really, because at this point we would have hired her whether she'd been armed, or toothless, or covered in blood—and then picked Dean up and cradled him while Helene went for a nap and I went to do errands that had been waiting for weeks.

It was quickly established that when Brenda was in the house, Brenda was in charge of Dean. She played with him, sang to him, got him to nap far more easily than we did, and dug deep into the drawers of gift outfits we'd received to dress him in the most unusual, colorful, even outlandish combinations she could devise.

While he napped, she folded his tiny clothes into the tiniest imaginable little squares. At the end of the day, she handed him to us cleaned and rested and fed, his nails clipped. The feeling we had for hours after she left became known in our apartment as the "Brenda High."

It would be exaggerating to say Brenda cured Dean of his crying. I don't remember when the screaming stopped, but eventually it did. Her calming tone certainly helped, as did Helene holding him on the couch in the evenings, sometimes all night. Whatever the pain was, or whatever the frustration was that he couldn't tell us about the pain—or ask us about it—finally faded. No more evenings being vibrated on top of the dishwasher, no more sixty-mile-per-hour midnight rides through the streets of Brooklyn. We may not have been able to ease the pain and answer, for ourselves at least, the question of what was causing it, but at least we had survived it. And so had he.

Dr. Sudhir Diwan is the head of the division of pain management at New York Hospital. He is an expert in all things pain—what causes it, which nerve fibers transmit it, and how to bring it under control. He grew up in a city in India named Ahmedabad, in the state of Gujarat, which is where, he notes,

Gandhi started his activities—"so this is a very well-known town in the world."

He was a surgeon and owned his own hospital in Ahmedabad, Diwan Surgical Hospital, but in 1988 he came to New York to study, and he became involved in the then relatively new medical field of pain management. He has stayed with it ever since.

I wanted him to answer one of Dean's more intriguing questions: "What would hurt more: getting run over by a car or getting stung by a jellyfish?"

Dean had asked me this when he was four, the colic screams long quieted, while we were standing on the dock of a little cottage we had rented on the end of Long Island. It was a little shingled summer house in a grove of trees. The dock jutted about ten feet into a shallow tidal estuary that was a favorite hangout for jellyfish: a globby red one languidly dragging red tentacles floated by as Dean asked his question. I noticed his eyes, already so large, widened even more when he wanted to know something. I laughed and said I didn't know, but made a mental note to write it down—it suggested such a wonderfully dark view of the world; it made me proud. I showed it to Helene, and to my parents. It was the first question asked by Dean that I looked for someone to answer. And I knew it was special because it lingered in my head after I'd committed it to computer keys:

What really *would* hurt more, getting run over by a car or getting stung by a jellyfish?

So I returned to the place of his birth, the place of my birth. I walked beneath the same gothic arches as I had that chilly November morning, as my father had on that temperate May evening, and along the same polished marble floors, the lobby and corridors busier with patients and white-coated doctors than they had been at 5:00 a.m. as I pushed Helene in a wheelchair, her hands clenched on the armrests. I took an elevator in the M bank up to the third floor and found my way to M 322D, to Dr. Diwan's tiny windowless office. After sitting down and waiting a minute while he finished a phone conversation, I repeated Dean's query.

"This is a very good question," he said, "because these are two completely different types of pain."

Dr. Diwan had a very, very thick Indian accent—for all I know, an Ahmedabad accent—and many of the words in the preceding sentence were initially difficult to decipher. He happily repeated words for me whenever I got confused.

"With neuropathic pain your nerves are irritated, so whether they are irritated by snake venom or a scorpion or a jellyfish it is pretty much the same. Some neurotoxins cause spasms of the muscles and some neurotoxins cause irritation of the nerves and severe burning pain."

So that's the jellyfish: neuropathic pain, pain coming straight from the nerves, traveling on the C fibers, which transmit constant burning pain, and the A delta fibers, which carry more sharp shooting pain.

Getting hit by a car, on the other hand, causes somatic pain, he said; that is, your bones are crushed, your muscles are torn, and these damaged parts transmit their own pain messages to your brain.

In other words, the jellyfish pain is pain for pain's sake, pure and simple, and the getting-hit-by-a-car pain is a side effect of an injury. Dean had asked about two injuries that represented the two types of pain a person could experience.

Dr. Diwan was careful to explain that Dean's question includes many built-in variables: the type of jellyfish, the location of the sting, the size and velocity of the car running over you.

For example, getting hit by a 2006 Hummer H2 going sixty miles per hour would surely cause more damage and hurt more than getting brushed by the jellyfish, a sea nettle, that Dean and I had seen.

But if it were a highly toxic bluebottle (*Physalia utriculus*) jellyfish, or a *Chironex fleckeri*—which, according to the *Medical Journal of Australia*, has caused sixty-three deaths since 1884—and the car were a Mini Cooper going, say, thirty-five miles per hour, then the equation would be much different. In those cases, and in cases where all the variables were more or less equal, it would be the pain itself, racing from nerve to nerve around the body, and not the pain stemming from the crushed bones, that could send a patient into shock and even result in death.

Dr. Diwan declared the jellyfish the victor.

We moved on to other issues: the worst pain either of us had ever experienced (he suffers from fibromuscular dysplasia; I had recently steam-scorched my hand while boiling water); how he came to be a pain specialist (a beloved professor had told him, "You will never understand pain until you feel pain"); and the larger issue of children and pain.

Here Dr. Diwan became quite expansive. To begin with, because their little bodies are all they know when they are born, whenever anything isn't quite right it takes on a somewhat exaggerated importance in their overall worldview. Treating pain in a child is one of the biggest challenges for Dr. Diwan and his colleagues, because children have such a tough time putting their pain into context. So they have the Wong-Baker Faces Pain Rating Scale.

Dr. Diwan stood up, shuffled some papers around on an upper shelf and handed me a xeroxed piece of paper. The Wong-Baker Faces Pain Rating Scale, which anyone who has ever accompanied a small child to an emergency room knows, is a series of drawings of six round faces, ranging from a smiling face to a straight-mouth face to a frowning face with multiple tears squirting out of the eyes. A doctor shows a child these drawings, and the child points to the one that seems to best represent the pain being felt.

The Wong-Baker Faces Pain Rating Scale. From Marilyn L. Hockenberry, David Wilson, and Marilyn L. Winkelstein, Wong's Essentials of Pediatric Nursing, *7th ed. (St. Louis, MO: Mosby, 2005). Copyright © Mosby. Used by permission.*

I looked it over closely. Strangely, the first person who popped into my head was not Dean but Helene: number two, the straight-mouth face, was actually quite reminiscent of her expression when she wakes up in the morning; the saddest face looked like she did when she gave that final push to get Dean out; and number three was not unlike a look she had given me a week earlier when I put an entire orange skin in the garbage disposal, jamming it.

"That looks like my wife!" I told Dr. Diwan.

"I do not understand."

"You know, when she had a baby." I pointed to the last one.

"Ah yes, this is very interesting that you say this, very interesting."

Labor pain, the pain of the birth of Dean and all the other children in the world, is the proto-pain, the über-pain, the base pain against which all other pain is measured. "That's what we compare pain with," Dr. Diwan said. "Not only is the intensity of it very high, but the frequency of that intensity is also very, very high. Everyone agrees that this is the worst. And this is what we start from when we want to know how much pain someone is experiencing, whether it be a child or not."

I thought of my mother: *"I remember that sitting was uncomfortable."*

And I thought of Helene: *"Like being turned inside out."*

Even with the epidural, by the end the pain must have been nearly unbearable. Probably way off the Wong-Baker Faces Pain Rating Scale. I remembered the tray of scissors and knives, the nurses and the young doctor, *Sabrina* on the television. I felt a little guilty for paying so much attention to the movie, and to Audrey Hepburn.

I thanked Dr. Diwan and started walking back to the office. It was a chilly March day. As I crossed the big avenues, I told myself I'd have to do better. Helene and I had two children and didn't plan on having any others, but I could still find ways to improve my behavior. I'd try not to put any more orange skins in the garbage disposal, and I'd never dillydally with the ice chips again.

"What would hurt more: getting run over by a car or getting stung by a jellyfish?"

—DEAN, on a dock on Long Island at sunset

Dr. Sudhir Diwan, director of the Division of Pain Medicine at NewYork-Presbyterian Hospital/Weill Cornell Medical Center:

"These two things are totally different: one is called somatic pain—the run-over injury—that means it's coming from the tissues, from the bones, from the cartilage, from the muscles. The pain secondary to injection of the venom of a jellyfish is most likely called neuropathic pain. That means the pain is coming because of the irritation of the nerve, and that could be generalized all over the body where the nerves are. That pain itself could be reason for shock and death. I would imagine the jellyfish pain would be stronger than the run-over pain."

"What does it feel like to get stabbed?"

—DEAN, after being prodded with a plastic Power Rangers sword wielded by his sister, Paulina, age two

Marianne Slack Wells, who was stabbed in the back with a hunting knife wielded by a deranged man on August 4, 1980, in Portland, Oregon:

"My first reaction was that somebody slammed me in the back as hard as you could with a fist; it just felt like that. I was seventeen years old, going to St. Mary's Academy downtown, waiting for the bus. The person who ran up to me afterward said, 'Are you okay?' I said, 'That guy just hit me in the back,' and he said, 'Well, he had a knife.' That's when I reached back and, you know, there's blood everywhere. It punctured my lung. I couldn't breathe, then I went into shock; I collapsed because I couldn't breathe. He was a really big guy; it was really more of a blunt force hit, no cutting feeling. Even now, anytime anybody will come up behind me, you know, to slap me on the back or something, I'm still pretty sensitive. It is a sort of fear-based adrenaline rush that happens to me. I get very anxious."

"How much of your body can you lose and still live?"

—ROBERT CHARLES REULAND, JR., age nine, Brooklyn, New York

Dr. Elliott R. Haut, assistant professor of surgery and anesthesiology/critical care medicine, Division of Trauma Surgery and Critical Care, The Johns Hopkins Hospital, Baltimore:

"The list of body parts that can be removed is long and varied. It includes the eyes, ears, nose, tongue, tonsils and even part of the brain. Abdominal organs that are not crucial include the stomach, small intestine, large intestine, colon, rectum, anus, adrenal glands, uterus, ovaries, pancreas and parts of the liver. Even both kidneys can be removed and replaced with dialysis.

"The most drastic extremity amputation is the interscapulothoracic—or forequarter—amputation, which includes complete amputation of an arm, including the shoulder girdle, shoulder blade and part of the collarbone. Advances in medicine can now save patients with two, three or even four limbs amputated at different levels. The term 'basket case' was originally coined to describe wounded soldiers with multiple amputations who needed to be carried in baskets.

"In 1950, Frederick Kredel, a professor of surgery at the Medical College of South Carolina, proposed the idea of a 'halfectomy' operation. This operation, now known as a hemicorporectomy, or translumbar amputation, is probably the most dramatic surgical operation performed. The surgeons remove the entire lower half of the patient's body, including both legs, the entire pelvis, the internal and external genitalia. This results in approximately fifty percent decrease in body weight. He suggested it be used only in severe cancer cases in which standard surgical procedures were not feasible or appropriate.

"The first attempt at this operation was performed in 1960. However, the patient died shortly after the operation. In 1961, the operation was performed on a twenty-nine-year-old patient who lived nineteen years after the operation. Since then, approximately fifty such operations have been described in the medical literature."

"Why do growing pains hurt?"

—LUCY BARRY, age six, Purdys, New York

Dr. Maurice Chianese, pediatrician, Lake Success, New York:

"The current theory is that bones are surrounded by a connective tissue, a lining, which tears as the bones grow, and it is the tears, we think, that cause the pain. It tends to be in the long bones, and it tends to be after periods of vigorous activity. It is a mild pain, kind of like a mild toothache, so you don't notice it while you are playing. One of the keys is that you feel a lot of pain before you go to bed, but in the morning everything is back to normal. Tylenol works, but a little parental massage works just as well."

"When you have a brain freeze, does your brain actually freeze?"

—SABINA MARINO, age five, Brooklyn, New York

Dr. Arthur L. Day, director, Cerebrovascular Center, Division of Cerebrovascular Surgery, Brigham and Women's Hospital, Boston:

"No. The brain doesn't have any sensitivity at all. It is covered by structures that protect it, to warn it when it is in danger of being penetrated. The pain structures are located in the scalp and skull and the outermost covering of the brain, which is called the dura mater. It means, literally, 'tough mother.' When you get cold, like a taste, it overwhelms the area of the mouth where the taste is coming from; it refers pain to adjacent things, to the nerves that go up, to the nerves that surround the brain, to the dura mater. So when you get this feeling of 'Gosh, that's painful,' it's not the brain complaining."

"Why is my blood warm?"

—DECLAN GUNN, age four, Brooklyn, New York

David Hillis, Ph.D., Alfred W. Roark Centennial Professor in Integrative Biology, University of Texas at Austin:

"All living things have a temperature at which their bodies work best. That is called an 'optimal temperature.' Many animals behave in certain ways to try to keep their bodies near the optimal temperature, so that their bodies will work well. Mammals, birds and some reptiles and fishes retain the heat that their bodies generate, and have various kinds of insulation (like hair, or feathers, or layers of fat) to keep it from escaping. Some mammals (including ourselves) also sweat on hot days to cool our bodies through evaporation. We also shiver when we are cold to generate more heat. In these and other ways, we keep our bodies at about the same temperature all the time, winter and summer, as do most mammals. Most of the time, that temperature is warmer than our surroundings, so we think of our bodies as 'warm.' Our insides are all about the same temperature, not just our blood, but we are more likely to feel the temperature of our blood than other internal body parts.

"Different animals have evolved different optimal body temperatures, depending on where they live. There are fish that live in Antarctic waters that have optimal body temperatures near (or even below) the freezing point of fresh water."

"Why do your hands and feet get wrinkly in the tub, and not the rest of you?"

—DEAN, in the tub

David Blaine, magician, who spent 177 hours submerged in water—the longest uninterrupted full submersion ever recorded—in a 2006 stunt called Drowned Alive:

"Your skin is made up of three layers: the outer, the epidermis, produces an oily substance called sebum—you can see the sebum when you touch a mirror or a window or something; it's the oil you leave there. Sebum keeps water off your skin, but after a long period of time in water, the sebum is washed off and the skin starts to absorb water.

"When you are immersed for long periods of time, dead keratin-filled cells in the outermost layer of your epidermis—which is called the stratum corneum, which protects the body from the environment—absorbs the water. This causes the outermost layer to have a greater surface area. Because it is attached to the tissue below, it wrinkles to compensate for the greater surface area. The stratum corneum is thicker on the palms of your hands and on the soles of your feet than on the other parts of your body because of the amount of wear and tear that your hands and feet get—imagine running with the skin on your stomach instead of with the skin on your feet. Because it's thicker, it absorbs more water and the wrinkling is much more noticeable."

ME: *"I guess your hands got pretty wrinkled after 177 hours underwater."*

"Look, every doctor I spoke to—some of the top people, people at NASA—said it was extraordinarily dangerous on your skin, your skin is going to fall off. The truth is, the skin was the quickest to recover, but having it absorb that much water was actually very painful, insanely painful. Your skin is not supposed to absorb that much."

"Pain? They didn't feel just, you know, super-wrinkly?"

"Oh, the pain was ridiculous. It was as intense as it gets. It started, I guess, thirty-six hours or two days in. You can't use your hands and feet: it would be like walking on an open wound. When I was in the tank and I would take the gloves off, people would gasp and scream; it looked very abnormal. I knew the pain would be bad, but the pain was unbearable."

"Why are people ticklish, and why sometimes are they not ticklish?"

—ADELLA MAY DZITKO CARLSON, age seven, Woodbury, Connecticut

Dr. Charles Sophy, pediatrician, medical director for Los Angeles County Department of Children and Family Services:

"Ticklishness is rooted neurologically. Being tickled is a perceived attack, so however you muster up your defenses is how you will respond to that attack. If you are someone who is a little stiff, someone who is in control, you will have more ability to ward it off and not giggle as much. If you are somebody who is emotional and able to talk about your feelings, then you are going to be tickled more easily. If someone is going to tickle you and you don't want to laugh, then close your eyes and focus on something else. Then you won't have that neurological reaction inside of you."

"Am I allergic to metal?"

—DEAN, apropos of nothing

Dr. Anna Nowak-Wegrzyn, assistant professor of pediatric allergies, Mount Sinai School of Medicine, New York City:

"It is extremely unusual to be allergic to metal. I would say no. The most common type of allergy to metal is a contact allergy. You see it in people who wear jewelry or are in regular contact with a certain metal. One example is nickel. Women who wear earrings, they sometimes become allergic to the nickel in gold or silver. So they might start to have itchy rashes or swollen ears whenever they wear earrings. For a child, a metal allergy would be a rash around your belly button, because you might have a belt that has a metal buckle, or metal buttons, so you would have the rash when it touches your skin. So if he doesn't have that, I would say no."

"Why do we have eyebrows?"

—CAROLINE BEAIL, age two, San Diego, California

Aaron E. Hirsh, Ph.D., professor of evolutionary biology, Stanford University, California

"In his surprisingly weird book *The Expression of the Emotions in Man and the Animals,* Charles Darwin notes that human eyebrows are descended from other mammalian eyebrows. This gets a little personal, but you know every once in a while, an eyebrow hair is incredibly long? Well, Darwin maintained that those real reachers are the vestigial remnants of the scattering of really long hairs one finds in the very same place on other mammals, including chimps and (easier to check) dogs. But why were eyebrows preserved, while most of the rest of our hair was lost? Darwin thought they were subject to sexual selection. He generally attributed most human traits that get a lot of grooming attention to sexual selection, which seems plausible enough. My own guess, however, would be that they're important for forming facial expressions that are more easily legible by other individuals in one's social group. Social interactions can have huge consequences for fitness: if a facial expression that is meant to convey 'Get away from my meat' is misunderstood to mean 'Here, have some meat,' there could be needless costs of time, energy and risk. Maybe eyebrows make such misunderstandings less likely, by accentuating expressions. One could test this, of course, by shaving a person's eyebrows and testing if he or she is harder to understand. Also, there are regions of the brain that respond exclusively to faces—and even to certain facial expressions—so one could watch whether they respond less sensitively or reliably when eyebrows are removed."

"Why does soap sting your eyes?"

—GABRIEL SCHLACHET, age five, Brooklyn, New York

Dr. Barbara Huggins, pediatrician, professor and chairman of the department of pediatrics, University of Texas Health Center at Tyler:

"It is related to the difference in pH of tears and soap. The pH of a solution is the way we tell whether it is an acid or a base. The lower the number, the more acidic; the higher the number, the more basic. Because the pH of the eye is about 7, it falls in the neutral range—neither acid nor base. Therefore, anything that has a really different pH that gets into the eye changes the pH of the eye, causing it to sting. The pH of soap or shampoo is 9.0 or 9.5, which makes these cleansers a base; but if you splashed vinegar (an acid with pH around 3) in your eye, it would also sting, because of the pH changes. The pH can be anywhere from 1 to 14, and the middle of that scale is 7. That's about where the tears fall. A lot of the systems in the body have neutral pH. They work the best that way."

"How and why do our ears make earwax?"

—DEVON CERMELE CINQUE, age four, Mountain Lakes, New Jersey

Dr. Stacey L. Ishman, pediatric otolaryngologist (ear, nose and throat doctor), The Johns Hopkins School of Medicine, Baltimore:

"About sixty percent of your earwax is made up of dead skin, and the rest of it is divided between secretions from glands in your ear: one of them is the ceruminous gland, and that secretes a protein-like substance, and there's a sebaceous gland, and that secretes something that is a lot like fat. And all of those things mix together to become earwax. And the reason that you make earwax is that it carries the dead skin out of our ear. We need it to carry the skin out of there as we make new skin. Also, it helps trap dirt in your ears and bring it out, and it helps repel water. And then there is some question about whether it actually has an anti-infection property, whether it can fight off bacteria and fungus."

"Why are people different colors?"

—REBECCA GUDZY, age six, Montclair, New Jersey

Jayne S. Gerson, Ph.D., anthropologist, former adjunct professor at Rutgers University, Camden, New Jersey, and senior conservation associate at the Philadelphia Zoo:

"Skin color is adaptive, reflecting a balance between conflicting needs. Exposure to the ultraviolet rays of the sun destroys folate—a B vitamin vital to successful reproduction—but is needed for the body to make vitamin D. Closer to the equator where sun exposure is stronger, it is more important to block ultraviolet light to protect folate—and ensure successful reproduction—and hence skin color is darker. As you move away from the equator to less sunny areas, insufficient vitamin D is a problem and evolution favored lighter skin color.

"Early human ancestors, living in the tropics, probably had light skin and dark hair. When they lost their hair, they evolved dark skin to protect folate levels. As early hominids moved to less sunny areas, their skin lost some of its pigmentation and lightened to allow sufficient vitamin D synthesis."

"How many hairs do I have on my head?"

—ROSA SCHEMBARI, age five, East Stroudsburg, Pennsylvania

Sy Sperling, founder, Hair Club for Men:

"I started about twenty years ago, and I'm still counting. Seriously: the average adult has about one hundred thousand hairs, or hair follicles, and children have the same amount. Redheads actually have fewer because their individual strands are thicker. Keep in mind, I am more in the business of replacing it when you lose it than an expert in hair when you have it, although I know a lot about hair."

ME: *"I guess a lot of kids didn't go to the Hair Club for Men."*

"It's extremely rare for kids to lose their hair. Usually it will happen in their twenties, or their thirties or forties, depending on genetic code. I started a foundation called The Hair Club for Kids about twenty years ago. At first we started doing a few kids with cancer, who lost their hair, at no charge. It became more and more. When I sold the company about six years ago, I think, we were doing up to a thousand kids a year at no charge. We would give them something that would work for them—whether it was a fitted wig, or a weaving process or a fusion process."

"What's inside my eyeballs?"

—MATTHEW CECCIO, age four, Jersey City, New Jersey

Dr. Don Lyon, chief of pediatrics and binocular services, Indiana University School of Optometry:

"There's a jelly-like substance that is called the vitreous humor. This substance helps give shape to the eye and allows light to get to the back of the eye so we can see. Before we are born there is also a blood vessel system that runs through the chamber where the vitreous humor is, but that blood supply goes away during pregnancy. The vitreous also helps keep the retina in place. The retina is a layer of tissue that is responsible for how we see; people make an analogy to the film in a camera. We also have a lens that acts as any lens does—it helps to focus light so we can see clearly. And then there is a nerve on the back edge of the eye. Basically, the nerve takes all the information from the lens and the retina—also from the cornea, but that's on the outside of the eye, and that's not part of the question he asked—and then sends it on to the brain to allow us to see our world."

"Do nose hairs turn gray?"

—CLAIRE MULLANY, age twelve, Brooklyn, New York

Giovanni Cafiso, age sixty-seven, who recently moved back to Pozzallo, Sicily, after running a one-man barbershop on the Upper East Side of Manhattan for forty-five years:

> "Yes, they do, but they turn gray later than the hairs on your head do. The hair in your ears and in your nose starts growing when you are forty or forty-five years old. Hair on your head usually starts getting gray before that. People always want me to trim their nose hair, otherwise, they look like a little elephant, or a little mouse, with all that hair there. I do it with small scissors. First, I dip them in disinfectant: you don't want the scissors to touch the nose, but if they do, if you have an accident, you want everything to be very clean. The hair in the ears turns gray, too, but people don't usually want me to cut that. I don't know why. They say, 'God made the hair grow in my ears to be like a filter, so don't cut it.' They just want me to cut around the edge of the ears, never inside."

We tell our kids not to swallow gum, right? And when they do, we look at them with alarm, or say, "Oh, Jesus." (At least my mother-in-law does.) But what's the harm? Does all the gum you swallowed in your lifetime collect in your lower intestine? Does it really take seven years to pass through you, as one old wives' tale has it? Finding the answer was surprisingly hard. I sought gastroenterologists. I asked Dr. Theodore Bayless at Johns Hopkins: "I have no idea," he said. I asked Dr. Michael Levitt of the Minneapolis Veterans Medical Center: "I assume it is not digestible. It doesn't plug you up or anything. But I really don't know. You should try Wrigley's."

"What happens when you eat gum?"

—GABRIEL SCHLACHET, age five, Brooklyn, New York

Steven Zibell, director, Clinical Research and Claims Support, Wm. Wrigley Jr. Company, Chicago:

> "Many people seem to harbor misconceptions about chewing gum, and we've received many inquiries over the years asking about the digestibility of our product. Chewing gum is made of five basic ingredients—sugar, corn syrup, softeners, flavors and gum base (the insoluble part that puts the 'chew' in chewing gum). The first four ingredients are soluble and are extracted from the gum as you chew. Although gum base is not intended to be swallowed, if it is, gum base simply passes through one's system, similar to roughage. This normally takes only a few days. Incidentally, chewing gum is a food product, so all ingredients used in it are in compliance with U.S. Food and Drug Administration regulations."

4.

Boys and Wheels

The windows of our apartment look out on New York Harbor and downtown Manhattan. It's not a skyscraper-eye view but a rooftop view: we are below the tops of the big cranes at the container port, at about the height of the wheelhouses of the freighters that bring sacks of cocoa beans from the Ivory Coast. At night the harbor is dark except for the lights on the piers, and on the ships, and off in New Jersey; early in the morning it is a black-and-white photograph in a hundred variations of gray.

Above and below is the weather, the clouds on a windy day rushing above green water rough with whitecaps. You can see storms coming from the west, black smudges that grow until they take over the sky. You can feel the first winds of a cold front rattling the windows. One evening we saw a rainbow over New Jersey, the arc landing in the middle of the Bayonne Bridge.

I got used to the early view when Dean was an infant, never sleeping, always screaming, his mother in the bedroom with a pillow over her head. I held him in my arms as the sun came up. If it weren't for him, I never would have seen the harbor just as the sky becomes perceptible. Or an hour later, when the orange of the sun hits the Staten Island ferries, the first big ships coming in to unload and, as it did one December Sunday, the *Queen Elizabeth 2* arriving from England.

By the time we started counting Dean's age in months and not weeks, he began to focus on the foreground, on the streets below us. When the empty early-morning buses wheezed by, his eyes lit up. Same with the fire trucks returning to the nearby station house, or the private garbage haulers—their engines roaring, their brakes screeching, their long hoods lit up with strings of yellow lights as they emptied Dumpsters as noisily as possible.

He couldn't have been more than one when he started picking out PT Cruisers and Mini Coopers and then our Honda Accord from the other cars on the street, sometimes from more than a block away. He was soon able to tell our Honda apart from another Honda Accord of the exact same year and color that also lived on our block—no small feat, especially to his mother, who was less adept at distinguishing between them, once even angrily trying to force her key into the wrong one. She thought our son was some kind of automotive savant.

But I was coming to understand: little boys just have an eye for things that move.

What sparks a child's first interests, creates questions before he or she can ask them? I had my phases when I was little, too, and they were also machines—cranes and, later, ships and airplanes. I had other obsessions, I know, childhood passions that faded away for no reason beyond the fact that I got older, but they've been lost to the fog of the last thirty-eight years.

Everyone in the family got excited when Dean chose trucks and cars as his first interest. This made gift-giving especially easy. His first birthday, his second Christmas and his second birthday were automotive extravaganzas: trucks, buses, cars made of metal, plastic and rubber filled his room. Someone even bought videos: scenes of groaning dump trucks hauling mountains of dirt, and cranes lifting girders, and hard-hatted workmen shifting gears, everyone bathed in clouds of dust, all set to a folk-guitar soundtrack. He was riveted.

Dean and my dad watched car races together. On Thursdays, the day Brenda took over for ten hours, a trip to a big four-lane avenue near us was always required. There he'd sit in his stroller, no matter the weather, his fingers pointing, watching the eighteen-wheelers go by. His favorite gift on his second birthday, given by my father, was *Mack: Driven for a Century* (Publications International, Ltd., 1999). We read it every night, the grand finale always the same and always satisfying: the 460-horsepower, twelve-liter E-tech engine-powered Vision eighteen-wheel tractor trailer.

Dean learned to imitate the *beep-beep-beep* of a reversing garbage truck in perfect pitch, perfectly timed. Vehicles made up his first words: truck was "uck" and bus was "bah." Though he was too young to ask questions, I could tell what he was wondering: Why are they so long? Why do they have so many wheels? Why do they go *beep-beep-beep*? Even "bah" was phrased like a question, his finger pointing, his eyes on me: *"Hey, do you see what I see?"*

Helene and I worried that we were giving in to sexist stereotypes by so enthusiastically encouraging Dean's love of trucks and buses. I became defensive: he had the whole harbor, the whole city to choose from—the towering clouds above, the massive ocean liners below, the airplanes, long celestial strings of them, lining up to land at Newark Airport. But he chose dump trucks. What could I do?

Boys just love things that move.

Helene thought we should give him other options. We bought him a toy kitchen of red, blue and yellow plastic, with a play oven, microwave and burners. This did distract him, for a while. He'd mess with the pans, slam the oven doors, mix imaginary recipes. It was an interest I encouraged: I can think of nothing better in my old age than having a son who runs the kitchen of one of the hottest restaurants in the city, a place of estimable charm with a kitchen of considerable merit. We'd always be guaranteed a table.

But the kitchen wasn't enough.

Helene bought Dean a girl doll.

She had blond hair and a blue-checked dress. I winced a little when Helene showed it to me, but figured I'd let nature take its course. I'm secure enough to have a son who plays with dolls, I really am. I stuck to my line even when a police officer friend of ours mocked me for allowing this to happen. I assured him I had my limits: had Helene come home with a glittering gown and a golden tiara for my son, or a pink tutu and slippers, or a fitted black dress with lace on the sleeves and along the hem, and a set of castanets, then I definitely would have put my foot down.

But the cars ran over the doll as Santa ran over the tooth fairy in my childhood. She was ignored, even neglected. It was the kind of thing that the city's Child Welfare Department might have called "parental abandonment" or "severe neglect." Little blond blue-checked-dress girl was not fed, or cuddled, or bathed, or taken to the imaginary doctor to cure any imaginary sickness or have an imaginary checkup, or cared for in any way.

Eventually, we found her in the microwave.

Dean's car and truck obsession obsessed me, so I decided to get to the bottom of it. Surely, I figured, someone had a theory. Searching back twenty-five years, I found just the right person.

In my first semester in high school I sat next to a girl in geometry class named Gia Rosenblum, who managed to be very cute despite wearing giant glasses and having a mouthful of braces and a spectacular amount of hair tumbling from her head, as was the style at the time. She was also smart and funny, so much so that for the first and last time in my life I looked forward to math class.

We whispered to each other outside the teacher's gaze, and cemented a friendship that lasted through high school and college. After that, our encounters became less frequent, but I still looked forward to them: Gia laughed more easily at my jokes than almost anyone I've known before or since. That's something you don't forget.

I went into newspapers and she kept studying, first for a master's, then for a Ph.D. She moved to New Jersey and got married. A psychologist, she focused on issues of child development. I figured Gia was the best person I knew who could explain Dean and his love of trucks. I called her and told her my mission. We agreed to meet and I hopped the train, New Jersey Transit's 6:11 local on the Northeast Corridor line from Penn Station.

After joining hundreds of commuters in a mad scramble through the concourse when the departure gate was announced, I watched from my window seat as we traveled beneath the

Hudson, through the grassy, stream-divided Meadowlands and the deserted and crumbling brick factories outside Newark, their loading docks long unused, and then through the little downtown of Elizabeth, its main avenue crowded with people going home from work. The industrial landscape gave way to more suburban vistas as we neared my stop, Metuchen.

Gia picked me up at the station: she looked remarkably as she had twenty years earlier; if anything, she looked better—a phenomenon I've noticed in many women who were forced to endure early 1980s fashions when they were teenagers. We caught up on this and that—her daughter Genevieve is a little younger than Dean—as she drove us on the final leg of my journey, to a Latin-fusion restaurant in downtown New Brunswick called Nova Terra.

I can think of few more enjoyable ways of doing research than drinking a caipirinha and sitting at a table with an old friend who likes to laugh at my jokes. Also, it was rodizio night, so we were free to eat all the meat we could for one price.

I started explaining about Dean. I felt the need to establish that Helene and I had never forced car-themed toys on him; in fact, we'd bought him a kitchen and a doll. It was a pretty defensive opening. She listened closely, laughing and smiling here and there. Then she warned me: whenever anyone in her profession talks about gender differences, a backlash is almost guaranteed. Could I handle a backlash? I said I could.

"At birth, like thirty-six hours after they are born, there is a difference in what boys and girls will pay attention to," she said. "Boys are more likely to pay attention to a sort of mechanical object, and girls will pay more attention to a human face. By age seven, kids will categorize things by gender like an adult would—what's a boy's profession, what's a girl's profession, what's a girl's toy, what's a boy's toy, what's a girl's trait, what's a boy's trait . . ."

I asked: "Is that because we're projecting that on them?" I thought of the cars and trucks Dean had received as gifts, the videos, and *Mack: Driven for a Century*.

Gia nodded. "If at thirty-six hours old babies are already expressing different preferences about what they are going to pay attention to, then you layer on top of that the fact that society bombards them with stereotypical messages about what's right for boys and what's right for girls, it becomes impossible to separate those two things."

She told me how she once went through all the hand-me-down clothing friends had given her when Genevieve was born, and how those that came from friends with little girls were covered with objects—flowers, butterflies, princesses, fairies—while the clothes from little boys were covered with occupations, like astronauts and firemen. She paused briefly while a waiter came over with a huge cut of lamb on a spit and carved off a few slices for us.

I took advantage of the pause to get us back on track—I wanted to know about boys and trucks.

"Well, there are definitely differences in what male brains and female brains seem to be designed to pay attention to."

"Uh-huh."

"One theorist describes the differences between male brains and female brains this way: that for some reason, male brains have a drive to understand systems—mechanical systems, organizational systems, structural systems. Those are the things that mechanical objects like cars and planes and Tinkertoys and Erector sets all provide, the opportunity to figure out how the system works."

I thought of the kitchen with its microwave and oven (systems) and of the girl doll (no systems). Trucks and cars and buses, on the other hand, had all those spinning wheels—

especially the 460-horsepower, twelve-liter E-tech engine-powered Vision—and made an incredible racket as they banged over potholes and spewed exhaust everywhere. Their systems were on dramatic display.

Gia moved on to the second part of her explanation. "Girls' brains seem to have the drive to understand the way interpersonal interactions work, and to understand the way that emotions work and understand the way that people relate to each other."

"Okay, okay," I said. "We think that this is so. But do we know *why* it is so?"

She took a sip of her mojito.

"The evolutionary theorists would say there had to be some survival value for males to have one particular strategy and females to have another one, because that's what they got selected for."

I picked up this thought: "So the boy who could tell his Honda apart from another Honda of the same make and year and color—"

"Got to mate with the girl!" Gia said, finishing my sentence.

When we first looked at our apartment before Dean was born, I got excited about the view because of the ships moving across the blue water through the open window frames. The real estate agent yammered on as I gazed out the window at longshoremen heaving ropes off bollards and tossing them into the water. I convinced Helene we should buy the apartment with the view and not a bigger apartment on a lower floor, something I came to regret a little bit when I realized how much noise a tiny screaming baby could make, and when my mother-in-law, having returned, became a semipermanent part of the household.

Ships were a bigger deal when I was a kid, when ocean liners still docked in Manhattan and still merited complete chapters in children's books devoted to machines that moved. Their size, not their speed, made them inspiring. In my grade school, we sang a song about the *Titanic* going down. I visited relatives on sailing days: my great-aunt Jane on the *Cristoforo Colombo* bound for Genoa; my grandmother Nonna, sailing to Romania on a freighter for a vacation.

After two years of trucks I decided it was time for Dean's first obsession to make way for something else. Through it all, the ships had sailed back and forth outside our windows. Now it was time to pay attention.

We watched as a big green-hulled freighter from Saudi Arabia navigated the shipping channel on one of those windy green-water days, a gang of tugs helping it pirouette. We watched tankers come and go. We watched the little yellow water taxis fight the current.

Then, four years later, a ship was front-page news: the *Queen Mary 2* arrived in New York City on her maiden voyage.

I had followed the news of the liner's construction for years. Then I told Dean this huge new ship was coming the next morning, and we agreed we'd get up early to watch. At 5:00 a.m., the harbor in that early orange phase, I went to get him and he popped right up. We put coats over our pajamas and headed to the roof, where we joined other fathers and sons. The morning was moist and cool, but the warmth of the sun suggested it was going to be a hot day.

It was hazy to the south, but then the liner's shape came into view, materializing all at once. It was an apartment block on the water, so tall with decks that it made the *Queen Elizabeth 2* look like a low-slung racing yacht. Ahead of it, a fireboat sprayed a towering plume of water, the traditional New York City greeting for a ship's maiden visit.

Now Dean looked beyond the garbage trucks and fire engines and early-morning buses, over the blue water and beneath the dissolving clouds. He borrowed my binoculars. As the liner passed behind Governors Island, it blocked the Statue of Liberty before disappearing behind downtown Manhattan.

"Whoa, that was big," Dean said. "It blocked the Statue of Liberty."

He was sold. In our apartment the *Queen Mary 2* became a measurement of size, of displacement and height, against which all other giant objects were soon measured. Is it bigger than the Empire State Building? What if you stand it straight up?

Two years later, the *Queen Mary 2*'s berth was moved to Brooklyn, right outside the windows on the left side of our living room. It is not the most elegant ship, squarish and stacked high as it is with balconies, yet there is something powerful and even graceful in its sheer black hull and towering red funnel.

It's out there some mornings, filling the frame, the sun bright on all that white paint. It always sails around sunset. Dean and I watch from the roof or from a nearby pier that juts into the shipping channel leading to the Atlantic. I've promised Dean we'll take a trip on her someday.

"How old is the ship?" he asked me as we walked back to our Honda from the pier following one departure.

"Two years. Don't you remember: we went on the roof the first time she was here?"

"Why do you call the *Queen Mary* a she?"

"You know, I don't know."

"How many times has she crossed the ocean since they built her?"

"Hmmm. I'm not sure. Maybe thirty times a year."

"How old will the ship be when we go on it?"

"I don't know—maybe four years old."

"How many times will she have crossed the ocean by then?"

"I don't know."

"I guess there's a lot of things you don't know, huh?"

"Yeah, I guess so."

"Why do ships have round windows?"

—DEAN, looking at New York Harbor

Richard Burke, Ph.D., professor and chairman of engineering, Maritime College of the State University of New York, Fort Schuyler, the Bronx:

> "It's because round windows don't have corners, and corners are places where the steel frames of the windows could crack, and we are very worried about cracks in the steel structure of ships. A ship is like a building that is going through a constant earthquake because a ship moves around in the waves. And consequently the structure is always being stressed and strained, and therefore the corners of windows could be sources of cracks."

"Why do people race cars?"

—ALEXANDER GIVOTOVSKY, age six,
Litchfield, Connecticut

Sam Posey, retired race car driver, a fixture at major racing events throughout the 1960s and 1970s who placed in competitions as varied as 24 Hours of Le Mans and the Indianapolis 500:

"It is the joy of control. It is power without effort; it appeals to the lazy, the intuitively lazy—you get so much out of doing so little in a car. And then there is the prospect of this immense machine which can do so much, and you just sit there doing so little but it is the right stuff, and it adds up to this tremendous extension of what you do yourself, and it is such a high. You can see a glimmer in the street when you take a car through a turn and it feels good, that control over the arc and the resulting G-forces that comes from the vector of trying to turn—the car wants to go straight and you are sort of managing that slipping force. It is a sensual thing; it is a sensual act. I think it comes down to those points of power and control, of the lateral motion of the car."

"Why is the road always wet in car commercials?"

—DEAN, after watching one

Jim Lesser, executive creative director, BBDO West, the advertising agency for Mitsubishi Motors:

"The automotive industry is constantly on the lookout for ways to make cars look better on film, and one of the things you always have to contend with is that, in the daylight, concrete and asphalt look very gray and flat. So what you do is wet down the pavement, and as a result the pavement gets much more black, and it allows the car to pop off of it in photographs. When you shoot a car commercial, you actually have at least one large water truck to spray down the road. It looks like a street sweeper but it is a water tanker, and it has these little spray nozzles, and it wets the road. You then roll film and drive down the street, and it looks better. It is similar in movies: you've got to create a distinct look and make the place look somehow magical. There is a film called *Black Rain* with Michael Douglas. There are a lot of rain-slicked streets at night, and the purpose is to add mystery and depth and moodiness to the environment. With a car commercial, you are also trying to add moodiness and emotion, because we've all watched cars driving down the street every day of our lives and it's not all that exciting in real life."

"Why is red for stop and green for go?"

—WYATT HARTE, age three, Brooklyn, New York

Carl Andersen, manager of the Federal Highway Administration's Arens Photometric and Visibility Lab, Turner-Fairbank Highway Research Center, McLean, Virginia:

"Robert Stevenson, who was very active in the British lighthouse service, was looking for an alternative color to white—most lighthouses had a white beacon—because he was building a lighthouse near to one that already existed, and he was afraid that ships wouldn't be able to tell which lighthouse they were looking at. Of the light sources and colored glasses available at the time, he found that red was the next most intense light—that was the color that would be seen from the greatest distance. So red was adopted in maritime signaling as an alternative to white lights, and was later adopted by the British Admiralty in 1852 for the port-side running light on steam vessels.

"A vessel observing that red light at night on another ship had to yield right-of-way to that ship. Green was adopted for the starboard-side running light: vessels seeing the green light on other ships had the right-of-way. When railroads were developed, engineers adopted this existing system as meaning stop and go. Then as motor vehicles began to appear, engineers adopted railroad signaling. And in 1914 Cleveland installed the first red and green traffic control light. It had nothing to do with a perceived cultural reason. It just happened to be, with the technology at the time, the light sources at the time, and the glasses, that red provided the next best available light to white."

. . .

Children zero in on contradictions. Boys may be attracted to things with wheels, but it took a girl to notice an interesting fact about New York State driving laws: a child must be strapped into a booster seat in the family car until age seven, but not while riding in the back of a yellow school bus.

"How come you don't have to use a car seat in a school bus?"

—LUCY BARRY, age six, Purdys, New York

Nancy A. Naples, commissioner, New York State Department of Motor Vehicles:

> "Children under four years of age have to use car seats on a school bus. In 1987, the New York State Legislature passed a law that requires companies that build large school buses to install seat belts for each seat. The law says that all of your friends that ride with you on the bus, and your bus driver, too, have to wear seat belts. When you get on the bus, remember to put your seat belt on and wear it until the school bus comes to a full stop."

I appreciate Commissioner Naples taking the time to respond to little Lucy's query, I really do. But like many public officials or employees of major corporations who would only answer via e-mail, there is a certain blandness in her reply, as though it had been created by a committee. Also, I must point out, she didn't answer the question. So I went elsewhere.

Michael Butler, regional president, Automobile Club of New York:

"One-word answer: compartmentalization. The backs of school bus seats are high. The child can only go so far forward and backward in an accident. If they go back, the back of the seat will protect their head against whiplash. If they go forward, then they are going to have the same effect because of the seat in front of them. They can't go too far forward. Most buses today have to be equipped with a seat belt lap belt, which protects the pelvic area and keeps their butts to the break of the seat, which is where the bottom of the seat meets the back of the seat. In some instances in special-needs buses, they do have child seats for additional protection, but that's in a specialized situation, where there might be handicapped children. The typical accident in a bus would not involve a rollover; it would be a low-speed crash, and a lap belt is sufficient protection with compartmentalization because everything is soft all around the child. When I was riding a yellow school bus, the seat came up to the middle of your back and that was it."

"How many bullets does a machine gun shoot?"

—JOE ROSEN, age five, Montclair, New Jersey

Gunnery Sergeant William E. "Gunny" Bodette, Jr., Second Marine Division, Camp Lejeune, North Carolina:

"The M240G machine gun, the preferred machine gun for the Marine infantry, can fire 650 to 950 rounds per minute.

It's called the cyclic rate. We've got 50-caliber machine guns that can fire 450 to 550 rounds per minute. We also have another machine gun that is called the M249 SAW—squad automatic weapon—and that can fire 725 rounds per minute. Those are the basic machine guns that the Marine infantry uses. The only drawback to carrying a machine gun now is the weight of some of them. The machine guns that we use now are extremely accurate and they really do bad things to bad people. All Marines are cross-trained on how to use a machine gun. The standard issue for most Marines is an M16. That fires a three-round burst. They used to fire fully automatic, but we were wasting too many rounds to kill one enemy."

"Why do clouds make shapes?"

—JIO KAMATA, age six, while looking out the car window at clouds on the way home from school in Aizumi, Tokushima Prefecture, Shikoku, Japan

Gavin Pretor-Pinney, author and founder of The Cloud Appreciation Society, based in London, which has five hundred members in thirty-nine countries:

"Meteorologists divide the infinite varieties of cloud formations into ten basic types. Not all of them make shapes—some are just too blurry and indistinct to have any clear edges to them. But the ones that are best at it are the sharp-edged 'cumulus' clouds, which are the fluffy cotton-wool tufts you see on a sunny day. Cumulus often look like elephants. This is because these clouds can develop vertical towers, borne on rising columns of air called thermals. As the cloud reaches the ripe old age of ten minutes or so, its droplets can start to evaporate away at the sides, leaving a central trunk that curls upwards as it is blown along in the wind and looks like the trunk of an elephant. This might be why ancient Hindus and Buddhists believed elephants to be the spiritual cousins of clouds."

"Where does wind come from?"

—STEPHEN DiNISO, age ten, Floral Park, New York, on a windy afternoon

Jeff Warner, meteorologist, Penn State University, State College, Pennsylvania:

"The Earth, because it is a globe, heats unevenly; it does not heat the same at the equator as it does at the poles. That leads to the formation of zones of high and low pressure. At the ground, then, that difference in air pressure causes the air to start moving. Air has properties of a fluid, like water, and much like water wants to flow downhill, from high to low, air wants to do the same. So where there are areas of high pressure—meaning lots of air—air wants to flow from that zone of high pressure to a zone of low pressure, where there is less air or less weight of air. That starts the wind flowing. That motion of air at the surface is what you feel as wind. There are other things that happen that cause it to blow in certain directions—like the Coriolis effect, an apparent deflection to the right, in the northern hemisphere, of things that are moving above the ground that are not in contact with the Earth—but the main reason for the wind is the movement of air from high to low pressure, which is called the Pressure Gradient Force."

"Is a rainbow hot or cold?"

—EDIE STURMAN, age four, Los Angeles, California

Bryan Busby, chief meteorologist, KMBC-TV News, Kansas City, Missouri:

"I can see why the question comes up, since the colors in a rainbow cover the entire spectrum—from shades of 'red hot' to 'ice cold' violet. Remember the seven colors in order: red, orange, yellow, green, blue, indigo and violet. Take the initials from these hues, and it throws you back to your elementary school art class teacher's method for remembering the sequence—ROY G. BIV.

"Rainbows are caused by the sunlight reflecting off individual smaller cloud droplets—leftovers, if you will, after the rain. Each one of those droplets acts like a tiny prism, and breaks up the sunlight into the visible spectrum of color. In general terms, since a rainbow usually forms after the rain, and usually a rain cools the surrounding atmosphere, a rainbow would be cool to the touch, if you could grasp it in your hands."

"Does water have symmetry?"

—BRONWYN SELL, age six, Brookline, Massachusetts

Rebecca Campbell, artist, Los Angeles, California, whose paintings include numerous images of water, whether in a swimming pool or a black stream in wintertime:

"Yes and no, because one of the primary qualities of light and of water is that they act as mirrors of whatever their context is. Water in a lake is giant and vast and solid, almost, and water running down your body after a shower is fractured and moving and small. So in terms of symmetry I think of water as a reflection of whatever it is doing at the moment. A drop falling off the end of your nose is symmetrical: it reflects its environment and the journey it's taken; it has gathered itself into this droplet. The water around a person who has just fallen into water, and has dislocated water, is completely asymmetrical. In some ways, water is whatever you ask of it."

There are lots of jokes about why a ship is called a "she," most of them sexist, like this poem I've seen variations of above the urinals of nautical-theme restaurants and next to the bottles in nautical-theme bars:

We always call a ship a "she" and not without a reason,
For she displays a well-shaped knee regardless of the season.
She scorns the man whose heart is faint and doesn't show
him pity,
And like a girl she needs the paint to keep her looking
pretty.

I asked Robin Woodhall, a former captain of the *Queen Elizabeth 2*, and he piled even more variations on this theme, including: "When going into port she always heads for the buoys. She shows her topsides, and hides her bottom."

Finally, one of his successors took me seriously.

"Why are ships 'she'?"

—CLAIRE CURRAN, age five, Baldwin, New York

Captain Christopher Rynd, master of the *Queen Mary 2*, anchored off Cannes on the French Riviera:

"The old tradition is thought to stem from the Romance languages' word for 'ship,' which was always referenced in the feminine. For this reason, Mediterranean sailors always referred to their ship as 'she,' and the practice was adopted over the centuries by their English-speaking counterparts."

5.

Dean and the City

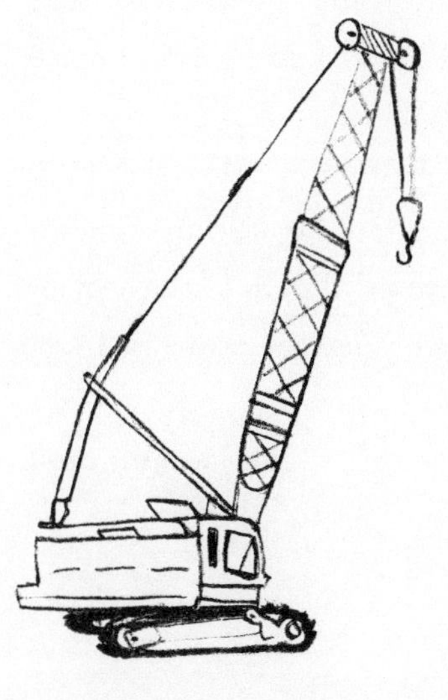

Having a son of my own made me wonder how my parents dealt with the challenges Helene and I faced now, and with my first questions. My parents were twenty-six; Helene and I were in our early thirties when we had Dean. They went out to a fancy French dinner a few nights after I was born; we got out for a quick drink a week after Dean got home, but all we could do was sit and stare at each other in exhausted, slack-jawed misery as our friends asked us what was it like, what was it really like, to have a baby?

Dean had tortured us in his first season. I was certain I had been a better baby. I asked my mother about this.

"You screamed for three months," she said.

I don't remember screaming. What do we remember from

Photo courtesy Walter Jamieson, Jr.

our first few years? Just a few disjointed images, some vague feelings and some surprisingly sharp snapshots.

I am four, it is spring, and the trees are just filling out. The cars are huge. I'm listening to the Beatles on bulky metal headphones, a record next to me spinning beneath a needle. A pretty babysitter with short brown hair is standing next to a tall piece of furniture with a mirror in it. I'm riding in a seat with folding red metal handles on the back of my dad's bicycle, and we're cruising through a park. It is summer, and the trees are full. I'm walking next to a river with my mother, the stones in the pavement little hexagons beneath my feet, the rungs of the black iron railing curving above me. I'm in our apartment: I smell perfume—Chanel No. 5—as my parents get dressed to go out, the light golden on the dark wood floors.

I'm standing on the sidewalk with my father leaning down toward me and talking.

Here is what he's saying:

"Wen, stick your tongue out."

"Why?"

"Just stick it out."

"Why?"

"Just stick it out."

So I do.

From out of nowhere he produces a piece of dry tissue paper. He wipes it against my tongue, and then furiously scrubs my face with it. He has done this many times before, but I'm still surprised. It makes me want to gag, this feeling of rough paper against my tongue, but it's soon forgotten as I experience the even more troubling sensation of having my own saliva used as a cleaning agent on my skin.

Then he lets me go back to what I'm doing, which is watching a crane.

Cranes were everywhere: the neighborhood of low-lying row houses where we lived in Manhattan was being knocked down, replaced by towering apartment buildings. Spindly towers of steel lattice slanted this way and that, lifting the city upward, and temporary wooden walls—in my memory they are yellow—lined the sidewalks, blocking the views of the vast dirt quarries that would soon be the basements of new buildings. My father would lift me up so I could see through the diamond-shaped holes created for the express purpose of giving little boys a peek at the mysterious world of dump trucks, bulldozers and backhoes rumbling up impossible inclines and spewing exhaust, and the nascent cranes just beginning their ascents.

We moved to Brooklyn from crane-land after my sister was born. This wasn't like going to the suburbs, where there was space and trees and lawns, but to another part of the same city where you could afford a house with lots of room because the neighborhood was dangerous.

Park Slope was run-down, but the houses were big and filled with elaborate woodwork and beautiful raised details in the plaster. My dad took me there on the weekends before we moved; I'd watch in awe as he'd knock down flimsy plasterboard walls with a sledgehammer and send squadrons of cockroaches scattering through the cloud of dust. On the big day, we drove that blue Volkswagen station wagon over the bridge with a round wooden table strapped to the top.

Here was one of the great sights for a crane-loving boy: off to the right rose the first tower of the World Trade Center, and atop it, four giant cranes. Whenever we crossed the bridge, I checked its progress. Up it went, and I wondered: How would they get the cranes down when they got them to the top of the new buildings, the tallest in the world?

Any New Yorker who was little when the World Trade Center was being built should remember seeing it grow, and the mixture of wonder and alarm it conjured. I used to puzzle about getting those cranes down, but also something else—the buildings were so high, could a plane hit them? My father reassured me that the towers were lit up at night to warn the planes away, the broadcasting tower on top had a blinking red light and, anyway, airplanes carried radar. Still, I remember a frisson of worry every time I saw them, first one and then the other, climbing a little higher and pushing those cranes farther toward the clouds.

When the buildings opened, we went to dinner at the restaurant on the top. We were so high up, the people on the streets weren't even ants. There were no people. There were no streets. The tables were on different levels, with brass railings between them, descending toward the windows, every one with a view.

That was an exciting night: we were tourists in our own city.

Little lights of humanity burned below us in buildings that rose from the earth like geometric stalagmites and in houses spread over the flatness rolling to the horizon. Rayleigh Scattering turned the edges of the sky pink and then red, tinting the railing next to our table and the white tablecloth. Then it was dark and it was like we were above a constellation of stars. It seemed at once reasonable and absurd that we were sitting so high up, nearly in the clouds, and that everyone else was down there.

The place where you grow up has a lot to do with who you are, and it holds a certain fascination for the rest of your life. I asked questions about New York City when I was little, and still do now. Would I be a different person if I'd grown up someplace else? Would I be more patient, or relaxed, or would the calm that I sense in many other places have calmed me to the point where I would cease to be the person I am? If I expressed my emotions in a foreign language, or even another accent, would they be the same emotions?

Children come to New York City and they ask about it: as adults, I guess, we just keep focused on our destinations, we rarely look up, but for a child the city is fertile ground for investigation, comparison and interrogation: Is the Empire State Building bigger than the Statue of Liberty? Was it hard to build the Brooklyn Bridge? Was it hard to build the Manhattan Bridge? What subway is fastest? What airport has the longest runway? How many lights are there in New York? Are there any dungeons in New York? And why on earth is New York called the Big Apple?

I was a city kid, but not the type who stood on a corner smoking cigarettes. I knew every crack in the sidewalk like a kid in the country knows the best hiding places behind the biggest trees. And yet sitting atop the World Trade Center that night, I was an outsider, as amazed as someone who had traveled half the world to sit at that table in the sky.

The events of the day were as much part of my childhood as the place where I lived. If I'd grown up in the 1940s, and not the 1970s, would I be the same person? Walter Cronkite described a strange world to a boy in footie pajamas: space shots and elections, assassinations and attempted assassinations, protests and more protests, bombings and wars, but not the kind I'd seen pictures of in books, with soldiers in blue or gray uniforms lining up in fields. These wars were in the jungles or the deserts, with helicopters, and men on stretchers.

I was often confused, and this prompted questions.

The Paris Peace Accords that got us out of Vietnam was signed on my father's birthday. We sat in the living room and watched a group of gray-haired men around a big round table sign pieces of paper.

I asked my mother what they were doing.

She said: "They're writing birthday cards to your father."

Then Watergate. Those hearings are so prevalent in my memory that I feel they must have been going on for several years. My dad and his father shared a sales office in Manhattan for their box-making company. I played with Civil War figures on the rug during the summer as my father watched the hearings on a small black-and-white television. At one point, the rebels routed, I watched along with him. I felt strangely sympathetic toward John Dean, who described the corruption within the Nixon White House, and looked very nervous and unhappy leaning into that microphone. He seemed, to me, like a kind person. Maybe he had a son and was a daddy, too.

"Is John Dean nice?" I asked my dad.

"Dean?" my father asked. "No, he's awful. They're all awful."

The hearings broke to a commercial. My dad explained, and not for the first time, what was going on: how a security guard had twice found tape covering a lock in this apartment building in Washington, and called the police, and how the burglars were arrested rifling through the headquarters of the Democratic National Committee and planting bugs (I pictured actual little bugs with legs). Some of the president's friends had been implicated, and surely the president would be, too, soon. My father mentioned the Plumbers, and the Committee to Re-elect the President (CREEP). It was all crazy because Nixon had gone on to win the election easily—why on earth did they have to break into the place?

But that was only one of many contradictions.

"Don't you think, Wen, if you were a burglar, and you were bugging an office, and you'd put a piece of tape over the lock so you could get back out and then it was gone, that you would have gotten out of there instead of just putting another piece of tape on it?"

"I guess."

"Of course you would: you're a bright kid."

I tried to picture myself, a six-year-old, my face recently scrubbed with my own saliva, bugging the headquarters of the Democratic National Committee.

One weekend my dad took me to his company's factory upstate, just the two of us. The place was filled with clattering machines cutting big sheets of cardboard into small sheets of cardboard. I sat in his office and counted the cars of a freight train that went by (the number 256 sticks in my head). We drove to Niagara Falls, where we took the *Maid of the Mist* right up to where the falling water hits the surface, and went deep into tunnels, boots and raincoats on, to see the waterfalls from within. We ate pizza in a little restaurant on the shore of Lake Ontario, gray and flat and impossibly big just outside the window, so amazing to me that you could not see the other side.

Still, even with this trip I didn't entirely understand what my dad did for a living. I knew the factory made boxes, and that those boxes held glass bottles of perfume, and that sometimes my mother wore that perfume, but it wasn't clear what my dad, watching the awful John Dean on television, had to do with it.

Back home, my teacher asked what my father did. I didn't give it a second's thought: I said he was an architect.

I'm not sure why I said that. Was I imagining the man who designed the World Trade Center? Was I picking up a habit of making up answers to questions? My mother had. (*"They're writing birthday cards to your father."*) Maybe I just wanted to describe a job I understood, one whose mission and result were clear. The teacher was impressed; I was very pleased. But when my father dropped me off the next day and she ran up to him and said, "Wendell says you are an architect!" I felt a peculiar sort of dread.

"Oh, no, I think he's pulling your leg," he said, smiling at me, and any embarrassment I'd experienced quickly faded as I tried to figure out what on earth "pulling your leg" meant.

I like telling Dean what I do for a living because it is so simple: I work for the newspaper. There it is, every morning, right outside the front door of our apartment. I prove this to him from time to time by telling him what's going to be in the paper the next day— "We have great pictures of a car crash: wait till you see it."

But sometimes he has unreasonable expectations. Maybe he thinks I have more power than I do.

He went over to a friend's house one afternoon for a playdate. The friend's parents were at work, and the babysitter was a little too ambitious inviting children over: there were eight or nine boys and girls in the house by the time she was done.

All was well and good, everyone running up and down the stairs and screaming, until three girls decided to break away from the maelstrom and have their own mini playdate within a playdate. They went into the parents' bedroom on the third floor, and locked the door.

The doorknobs in this house were very elegantly designed, the kind you'd see in a decorating magazine, with a tiny hidden latch above the knob to unlock it. But they are not designed to be handled by small children. So when the babysitter called them down to dinner, the little girls couldn't get out.

Shouting, the babysitter tried to explain through the door how to flick the latch. Dean and his chums ran around some more, screaming and yelling, stopping from time to time to offer advice. Finally, the babysitter called the fire department.

Now this was exciting. Sirens wailed in the distance, then closer. A pumper truck pulled up outside, lights flashing. A team of firemen came tramping up to the third floor weighted down by gear. They tried the lock. No luck. So one climbed into a harness. He went out through the window in the hallway and crab-walked on the ledge outside the house to the room where the girls had trapped themselves. He let himself in through the window and unlocked the door.

When I got home Dean wasn't as excited by this as one might think. He was very nonchalant. But he figured I knew all about it already.

"Is it going to be on the front page?" he asked.

I have a photographic road map to my own childhood: three albums of black-and-white photographs that my dad put together, and to which he obviously devoted a great deal of care, from the time he and my mother got married until I was ten, when they split.

At first, my parents are younger than I am now, my father in suits and ever-widening ties, his hair initially crisply cut and combed, and eventually with a stubbly beard in a jean jacket; my mother—many pictures of my mother—in miniskirts, boots, in big sunglasses like a model in *Vogue*. I'm playing with a dump truck in the sand, or wearing a blazer the day we went to see my great-aunt sail on the *Cristoforo Colombo.* My sister, head in her hands, smiles over her birthday cake candles.

But for every picture of our family is one shot somewhere in the city that had nothing to do with us: a rail-thin model on a runway in a short white dress; a horse-drawn carriage, flecked with snow, in Central Park; a woman in a raincoat and miniskirt in the Museum of Modern Art, an abstract painting in the background; a black kid looking out a bus window above a campaign poster reading "Our Judges Mustn't Be Picked in a Back Room," or the Beatles leaning on a podium and giving a press conference.

I've always liked the story of how my dad got those photographs of the Beatles.

This was 1966, the band's fourth time in America. *Revolver* had just come out. Since my dad worked with his father, he could more or less do as he pleased. So after reading that they would be giving a press conference, he put his camera in his pocket and walked to the Warwick Hotel, where thousands of teenage girls in short skirts, screaming and giggling and crying, crowded the sidewalks behind police sawhorses.

My dad saw some men carrying benches. He helped pick one up and he and one of the workmen carried it into the hotel, through the lobby into a large room with a lectern, where they put the bench down at the very front and my dad sat on it. A little time went by. The place filled up with reporters and photographers. And then the Beatles came out and took questions. My father didn't ask any, but he shot away, and now there they are, John, Paul, George and Ringo, smiling and leaning forward on the lectern to answer questions, John in a blazer with giant stripes, Paul in a paisley shirt, all of them with haircuts like mine at the time, ensconced forever in our family photo album.

I wanted to create a record like this for Dean, a portrait of a

Photo courtesy Walter Jamieson, Jr.

family and its city and its times—and those things that would be gone by the time he was my age. I started filling up albums with black-and-white photographs: Dean and Helene by the Hudson River; me in the newsroom of my paper, drinking coffee; the three of us and several of our friends, one wife pregnant, posing outside the little cottage near the tidal estuary on Long Island.

Like the Upper East Side in the late 1960s, our neighborhood along the waterfront in Brooklyn was changing. The working port that attracted those green-hulled container ships from Saudi Arabia was being phased out, and new buildings were going up, blotting out our view piece by piece. I wanted to record this evolving place.

I was copying my father, deliberately.

But I was starting to copy him in other ways, too.

One Indian summer day a rusty but evocative-looking freighter came in. I got my camera, and Dean and I headed down to the pier. It was hot and he wanted ice cream so we stopped at a little grocery store. As usual he eschewed the classics, like an ice cream sandwich or a Fudgsicle, and instead chose the most disgusting selection available, in this case a bright yellow

SpongeBob SquarePants bar with frozen globes of black bubble gum for eyeballs. By the time we got to the ship, which I shot through the chain-link fence, its crane swinging pallets of burlap sacks filled with cocoa beans, Dean's face was a glistening, slimy, lemony mess. But I was prepared: I'd grabbed about thirty napkins in anticipation. I leaned down to talk to him.

Here is what I said:

"Dean, stick your tongue out."

"Why?"

"Just stick your tongue out."

"Is John Dean nice?"

—WENDELL JAMIESON, age six, during the Watergate hearings

James F. Neal, attorney, Nashville, Tennessee, former chief trial counsel of the Watergate Special Prosecution Force:

"John Dean was my main witness. I spent a great deal of time with him. Of course, I put him in prison first; that was part of a plea bargain. I thought he was a very nice guy. He had a Saul-to-Paul conversion—you're not from the south, I can tell, but that's an expression: Saul was on the road to Damascus to persecute the early Christians, and then Jesus spoke to him, and he realized what he'd been doing was wrong, and he took up the name Paul and started making up for the things he'd done. So that's what Dean did: he said there is a cancer growing on the presidency. He tried to straighten things out. He tried to warn Nixon. Until we heard the tapes, I was a little skeptical of how bad things were, but when we heard them, it turned out everything that

John Dean was telling us was absolutely true. He was a fantastic witness, he's very bright, great memory."

ME: *"Did he have a sense of humor? Did he like practical jokes? Was he nice to his son and his wife?"*

"It wasn't a situation for much humor. Before he went to prison, he would come down to Nashville and meet with me. He was always very solicitous of his wife, Maureen. It was really hard work getting him prepared, and I didn't really have a chance to test his sense of humor."

"Why are there sidewalks on both sides of the street?"

—DEAN, on the way to school

Iris Weinshall, Commissioner, New York City Department of Transportation:

"It goes back to the late 1800s. The city started to grow, we didn't have a subway system, we didn't have an extensive mass-transportation system. How did people get around? If you didn't have a horse and buggy—which was very expensive—you walked everywhere. We started to think how to keep people safe. There were something like nine hundred pedestrian deaths at the turn of the century. Basically, what the government was saying was we have to recognize there are multiple uses for the streets, and we have to tell the property owners how to create this safe environment for people."

"If Mrs. O'Leary's cow knocked over a lantern in our neighborhood, would all the buildings go on fire?"

—DEAN, after learning a song at school about the Chicago fire

Salvatore J. Cassano, chief of operations, New York City Fire Department:

"No, they wouldn't. In the time of the Chicago fire, they had wood-shingle buildings and wood-frame buildings. In Brooklyn, if you take a look at the beautiful buildings, the brownstones, they are very well made, they have brick nogging between the buildings—spaces. We call them 'fire stops.' Very rarely, unless some work had been done, would a fire in a brownstone spread to the next building. They will spread vertically but not horizontally. Normally we call a brownstone fire a 'one-building fire,' as opposed to a fire in a wood-frame row house where we are playing catch-up, trying to confine that fire to the one building that it's in."

"How many lights are there in New York?"

—RONAN GALLAGHER, age five, Los Angeles, California

Peter Jacobson, lighting specialist for Consolidated Edison, New York City:

"There are many types of light bulbs used, including the incandescent light invented by Thomas Edison, the fluorescent lights used in schools and stores and new-light emitting diodes, or LEDs, that are very efficient and are in many of the traffic lights and Walk and Don't Walk signs in New York City. Lighting in general uses about twenty-five percent of the power Con Edison distributes. Electric power usage is measured in kilowatt hours, and a kilowatt hour of electricity would be enough power to light a 100-watt incandescent light bulb, the type found in your home, for ten hours. In 2005 Con Edison distributed 40,629,913,573 kilowatt hours of electricity to New York City, and assuming that a light bulb is on for twenty-five percent of the time and that on average the light bulb consumes 100 watts, then that amount of electricity would light 25,393,690 light bulbs."

"Are there any dungeons in New York City?"

—NICK MANSKE, age seven, Brooklyn, New York

Martin F. Horn, Commissioner, New York City Department of Corrections:

"There are people who commit crimes and we lock them up, but we don't use dungeons. If you were in one of our jails, your day would be pretty routine, but it wouldn't be like being in a dungeon. You would get three meals a day and a chance to work. You would probably be living in a dormitory with about forty other young men. About half of our inmates live in dormitories and only those that need to be apart are kept in cells. Your family could come and visit you several times a week, and you would be allowed to watch television sometimes. But you wouldn't get to decide whom you live near and with, and you wouldn't get to decide when you go to sleep and you wouldn't get to decide what you eat. We make all of those decisions for you. It is kind of boring, and it is not fun.

"If you went back to the 1800s, the common practice was to lock individuals in cells. Contact with other inmates was thought to be corrupting. They ate their meals themselves, they went outdoors by themselves. The experience was so isolating that many of them went crazy. The modern penal system really began at Auburn prison in upstate New York where the notion of solitary imprisonment was rejected in place of what we now call congregate care."

Me: *"How about 'The Tombs,' the jail in downtown Manhattan? I had a friend who had to spend the night there once; something to do with breaking into a car. Is that like a dungeon?"*

"No, no. That name has to do with the architectural design of the exterior of the original building, which was believed to be reminiscent of some Egyptian tomb. That building no longer exists. Now we call it the Manhattan Detention Complex. The newest tower of the center is a modern air-conditioned building that was built in the 1980s, and is probably one of the most humane jail facilities in the country."

"Why is New York called the Big Apple?"

—DECLAN KRISKA GUNN, age three, Brooklyn, New York

Edward I. Koch, mayor of New York City, 1978 to 1989:

"Harlem was called the Big Apple before New York City was, and it was intended in those days to convey that it was the jazz capital of the world. It was an expression used by jazz musicians. There's a showbiz saying, 'There are many apples on a tree, but only one Big Apple.' I don't know exactly when it shifted to the whole city, but eventually it did. I think there are other versions, but that's the one I accepted when I was mayor and related to people when they asked. Now, I could also say to you that New York City is the international capital of the world, of finance, culture, communication, commerce, and calling it the Big Apple conveys that."

"Why is the rat there?"

—ANTONIO PAPA, age four, East Williston, New York, after passing a construction site with a giant inflatable rat on the sidewalk, surrounded by men with placards

Stephen McInnis, political director, New York City District Council, United Brotherhood of Carpenters and Joiners of America:

"It is directed at the employer—he or she is the rat, not the workforce. We put it out there because the employer (a contractor or subcontractor on site) is paying substandard wages in unsafe conditions. Unions have always had picket lines, but they generally don't catch the public eye anymore. The inflatable rat is an attention grabber—people stop and look, they talk about it, they take notice. This works well especially at commercial properties: no one wants the rat in front of their building because it draws too much negative attention. The rat really rattles other tenants, who then complain to building management, who then may encourage the leaseholder to utilize quality union contractors. We've found it effective in various corporate campaigns as well."

"What was it like to live in the 1940s?"

—SAVANNAH KELLY, age five, Milpitas, California

Irene Stapinski, Jersey City, who was born in 1931 (and is my mother-in-law):

"It was great. I was a kid; I didn't take the war that seriously. I mean, my friends and I knew it was frightening, but we didn't really understand the bad part of it. We just knew that we were all cheering for the Americans and that the Nazis were bad. Everybody was so patriotic. We had all sorts of things going on in the neighborhood; they brought a captured Japanese submarine to Journal Square to help sell war bonds. If we went to the movies and we brought aluminum or pots and pans or rubber balls—anything useful for the war effort—we got in for free. I was fourteen when the war ended. There were parties in the streets for almost a year.

"After the war people started to have more money and live better. They were able to buy refrigerators and have gas stoves. I was sixteen when we got our first refrigerator—in fact, I bought it. Before that we had an icebox. I bought it when I went to work at Chase Bank in New York. I was a secretary. To go to New York was a big deal, a dream for someone who graduated from high school and wasn't going to go to college. After work we'd stay in town at least once a week. We'd shop, we'd go uptown, we'd go to the movies. We'd go over to Brooklyn to swim at the St. George Hotel. Nobody had a car so we didn't have to worry about driving. There was no fear of murders and everything else, like we have now."

"Why do you never see baby pigeons?"

—HALLIE SIFTON, age four, Brooklyn, New York

James F. Avery, co-treasurer and secretary of the National Pigeon Association, Newalla, Oklahoma, which was founded eighty-six years ago and has more than two thousand members around the United States:

"Because they can't fly, first off, and you'll never see them unless you go where they are nesting. In New York City, that's under bridges, signs—I've got pictures people have sent me of nests on fire escapes. Anywhere like a cave—eaves on houses, buildings. They don't want you to be able to walk up and carry off their eggs and babies; they've got to hide from predators, which in the city can be cats, dogs, hawks and people—the biggest one. I've even seen nests that are just a few twigs, really; the eggs will be just lying on the ground. They don't build a very good nest, pigeons. It might keep the egg from rolling off the ledge, see, but that's it. The squabs will be there three to four weeks before they can fly. You probably are seeing young birds, you just don't realize it because young birds are the same size as adult birds. If you see one out there chasing other pigeons around, it is a baby begging its parents to feed it. They can fly like adults, but they are only seven to eight weeks old."

"Mommy, why when you were little was everything black-and-white?"

—ISABEL PHILLIPS, age six, New York City, looking at pictures of her mother as a little girl in an album

Bob Shanebrook, photographic film products specialist (retired), Eastman Kodak Company:

"Even though there was some color photography before the turn of the century, black-and-white was much more prevalent up until the early 1960s because it is a much simpler process. Black-and-white is one image on the film and then on the black-and-white print. Color is a blue record and a green record and a red record—these three colors emulate the human visual system. Organic-synthetic dyes are needed for color film, and a lot of work was done with them around World War II: they wanted to do infrared photography, to take pictures through atmospheric haze. Then, after the war, companies had to figure out how to make the film in quantity, and how it was all going to work in the commercial developing and printing process. It took time. The main crossover from black-and-white to color film, commercially, was around 1964.

"But you know there is still a human need that is not fulfilled by color; some people still prefer black-and-white. Even if you look at the new digital cameras, many have a special button where you can take pictures in black-and-white.

Or you can print color pictures in black-and-white. There is still that aesthetic; people have a desire to have a black-and-white image."

"What's a record?"

—HILARY CARLSON, age seven, Litchfield, Connecticut, after being told by her mother: "You sound like a broken record."

Dick Clark, former disk jockey, and longtime host of *American Bandstand* and *Dick Clark's New Year's Rockin' Eve*:

"Long before there were iPods, MP3 players and CDs, there were records. A record was a sound that was preserved on a flat piece of vinyl that was then placed on a turntable that revolved at 78, 45 or 33 ⅓ revolutions per minute (RPM). A needle was then applied to it, and through amplification it reproduced the original sound that was recorded.

"Most records included music. When you stop to think of it, recorded music has become the 'soundtrack of our lives'—every moment we may recall, whether it be happy or sad, is accompanied by some music we listened to at the time. Though it was many, many years ago, I remember to this day the very first record I purchased: *I Can't Get Started* by Bunny Berigan. My first buy of a rock 'n' roll record was *Rock Around the Clock* by Bill Haley & His Comets. Since then I have accumulated thousands of individual pieces of music that encompass every conceivable type created."

"How many hours of TV will turn your brain into 'mush'?"

—ANNA GAWLEY, age six, Danbury, Connecticut

Jeff Zucker, President and Chief Executive Officer, NBC Universal Television Group:

"How much you watch is as important as what you watch and how you watch it. There's lots to watch on TV that is there just to be fun, and that is okay, but if you watch hours and hours of that and you lose the time you should be doing your homework or going out to play, then your brain might get very mushy. TV is just one part of the media. If you watch TV that informs you or stimulates you or excites you, or increases your understanding of the world, if you watch TV with your family and talk about the shows with them, then TV can actually be part of what makes your brain smart."

ME: *"You have four kids. What kinds of rules do you have for them and watching television?"*

"We let our kids watch TV as long as they've done their homework or taken their baths or done whatever else they need to do. Then they can watch some TV and have fun with it."

Kids pick up their parents' interests, or are at least interested in them. I may have been the only kid around with the Beatles in his family's photo albums, but practically everyone in my generation was raised with the Beatles on the turntable. Whether we stayed fans into adulthood or not, the band's music certainly touches us. And we pass this on to our children.

My friend Jere's daughter asked him a question that has long vexed him. I wondered who could answer it—a rock historian? One of the surviving band members? Perhaps even the chief suspect herself? I wrote a letter and put it in the mail as a long shot, but soon enough, an answer appeared in my in-box.

"Why did the Beatles break up?"

—ELLA HESTER, age eight, Brooklyn, New York

Her father, Jere:

"Yoko."

Yoko Ono:

"Because they all grew up, wanted to do things their own way, and they did."

6.

The Language of Life

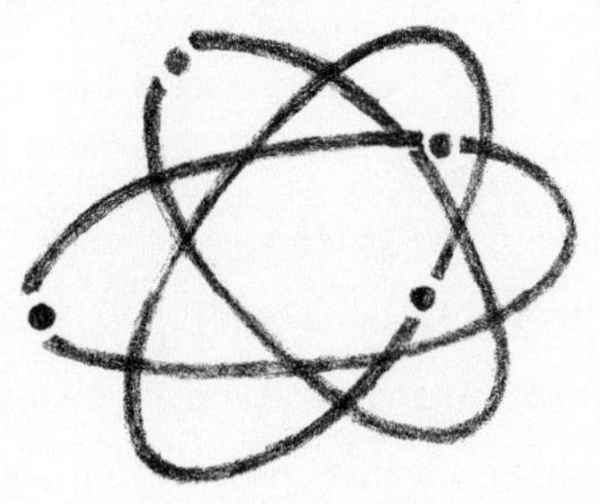

When I really think about it, when I'm feeling confident and everything is going well in my life, I truly don't care how much my children measure up to other children. It is not that important to me where they go to college, or what they end up doing for a living. It is only important to me that they be happy and that, like me, they find something they enjoy doing so their salary is not the main reason they go to work every day.

When I really think about it, that's how I feel. But it can be a challenge: the comparisons to other children are everywhere, the measuring-ups either obvious or subtle, and no matter how much I promise I won't play that game, sometimes I do.

It reminds me of when I was single and in my early twenties, with no girlfriend and none on the horizon, and everywhere I looked there were photographs of women in bikinis on the covers of magazines. Or of the dieter confronted with images and descriptions of food every time he or she turns on the television. You try to put it out of your mind, this thing that obsesses you, but you can't, because forces beyond your control put it right back.

It started just moments after Dean was born. The nurse whisked him away, touched him here and there, looked at his fingers and toes, and then announced that his "Apgar score" was 9. A second nurse wrote it down. "Does that mean he'll get into Harvard?" I asked. No one laughed.

This was the first of a million tests. The next came at the doctor's office, where Dean's weight, height and head circumference were compared with those of millions of other children around the nation. The computerized chart, longer with each visit, showed his height was average, while his weight was very low, in the fourth percentile, which upset his mother—from then on, she was not happy unless he was eating or had eaten very recently. I tried to reassure her by pointing out that he was holding his own in the head-circumference department, and was even a little bit advanced in this area. But this failed to comfort her. In fact, she started to worry that his head was getting too big.

The Apgar scores and the weight and head-circumference comparisons were only the beginning. You worry that your child isn't crawling on time, or walking, or toilet training, or tying his shoelaces, or drawing, reading or writing. You worry about how your child holds a pen, that he cries too easily, about how much he knows.

So I've come up with some self-defense mechanisms. When Dean ends up on top in these comparisons, that's great; when he doesn't, I can always rationalize.

Remember the boys who knew the inner and outer planets? Well, once the solar system was safely hung in Dean's room, signaling the end of our planet-identification period, my thoughts returned to them.

They were eggheads, I decided, obviously drilled so rigorously by their parents—morning, noon and night, perhaps even while they slept—that their social development was being stunted. They knew the planets, sure, but at what price? They were awkward and unhappy, mentally closeted in their little self-contained planet worlds, unable to interact properly with the children around them. Not only that, they were rude and unkempt, and were no doubt spiraling toward serious addiction problems. Hadn't one of them been arrested for knocking off a liquor store?

This made me feel better. Of course none of it was true. But you never know what the future holds. I can always dream.

Brenda taught Dean to put on his coat: she would put it on the floor, and he would flip it backward over his head. I was so thrilled the first time I saw him do this you'd think he had just recited a Shakespearean sonnet. Then my sister, in from Los Angeles for a week, saw the backward coat flip and said that she had been planning to teach her son Ronan to put on his coat this way, but that he had figured out on his own how to put it on "the regular way," so she didn't have to.

The regular way? I didn't say anything, but after they went back to the West Coast I found I couldn't get the notion out of my head. I obsessed about this for weeks. I tried to get Dean to modify his technique, to do one arm at a time sideways, but he resisted—he enjoyed the flip. Up in the middle of the night, thinking about everyone who had ever wronged me in my life, imagining the Planet Boys' life of crime, I nearly called my sister to curse her out.

It's not just coats or the solar system, it's everything. When you encounter a weak spot, you try to fill it.

"Do you know the seasons?" I asked Dean one late-winter morning when he was old enough that he really should.

"No."

"Oh, come on. You know the seasons. Tell me one."

"Summer."

"Right! And what comes next?"

"I don't know."

"Sure you do. After summer. What happens to the leaves on the trees?"

"They fall down."

"Right! So, what's that season? You just said it. What season comes after summer?"

"Fall down?"

"Not quite."

"Halloween?"

"Oh brother."

"What does 'Oh brother' mean?"

When you're the father of a little boy, which involves many joys, you do have one rationalization in your back pocket that is ready to be used roughly half of the time—that your little boy has the disadvantage of not being a girl. Girls just seem to be ahead of the game in so many ways when they are little; they are not as apt to tumble spontaneously off stools as boys are. We saw this clearly illustrated the first day we took Dean to nursery school: the little girls took off their coats and hung them up, neatly, and then went to help all the little boys, whose coats were half off, or still zippered and hopelessly tangled around their midsections, or attached to one hand and dragging along the floor.

This girl thing works all the time. My child-development friend Gia, in that noisy Latin-fusion restaurant in New Brunswick, not only gave me a lengthy explanation for why the two sexes were interested in different things, but also explained a few theories about why they learn at different rates. But I don't care why it's true, I'm just glad that it is.

A classmate of Dean's wants to go on the Internet when Dean has never heard of it?

No worries—she's a girl.

A colleague of mine brags about how her daughter is a green belt in tae kwon do while Dean's biggest physical activity is kicking air while watching the Power Rangers on TV, and occasionally injuring himself in the process?

Yeah—but she's a girl.

It's the most 100-percent-pure-gold boy-raising rationalization on which a father can depend.

Dean's friend Anna is standing in the school yard, doing her twenty-seven-times tables aloud while drawing a chalk schematic of Robert J. Oppenheimer's working model of nuclear fusion while Dean chases pigeons through a big puddle?

That's fine, just fine—I mean, hey, she's a girl.

But on that day when the rationalizations don't work, when you realize that for whatever reason your precious child is a little bit behind, it can be very painful. It was especially shocking for us, because Dean's problem was language and speech, and we are both writers. This wasn't an area we'd ever worried about. Sports, maybe, math surely, but not Dean expressing himself.

I remember trying to unlock the coded words of adults myself. My father, when telling a story or making an example, would refer offhandedly and often to Mr. or Mrs. So-and-so—leaving me to believe that this was the world's most popular last name.

For a child, words—their meanings, the subtle differences between them, and where they come from—are a puzzle, as are expressions whose origins are long forgotten:

"What does 'From the horse's mouth' mean?"

"What is the difference between joking and lying?"

"Why is it called 'kidnapping' if you can steal away adults, too?"

In the beginning, with Dean, combinations of words seemed like a distant goal. Just understanding the few he knew was a struggle.

This was just before his second birthday. He had started to spend time with other children at a mommy-and-me class in the neighborhood. It was on Thursdays, the one day we had Brenda, so Helene hadn't gone more than once or twice. The class was taught by a woman named Rianne, who had a daughter about Dean's age.

Rianne happened to be an ex-girlfriend of mine. We dated when I was a senior in high school and she was a junior. She went to a different school than I did, a much bigger one, and was generally considered to be the prettiest girl there. She had deep brown eyes and was easily one of the kindest people I've ever known. We spent endless hours in each other's houses, saw Elvis Costello play solo, got lost in the middle of the night in the lower level of Rockefeller Center in Manhattan when it was closed to the public. She was even kind—though surprisingly firm—when she dumped me, which she did on the front steps of her house about two months before I went to college.

This is a danger of living in the same place your whole life: you or your wife occasionally bumps into your old girlfriends, and in surprising places. Helene met Rianne when she became Dean's first teacher. She encountered another old girlfriend, who shall remain nameless, in the locker room of the gym, where both were naked. "She's got some big boobs, that girlfriend of yours!" Helene said later that evening, recounting the events and sights of her day.

I'd also see Rianne around the neighborhood. She'd update me on Dean and Brenda and the mommy-and-me class. She was infectiously enthusiastic, just like she had been in high school.

Then Helene saw her one afternoon while they were racing around the neighborhood, strollers in front of them. Rianne was uncharacteristically solemn. She said she was worried about Dean's vocabulary, that he didn't seem to have enough words, and that those he did have were hard to understand. She thought we might want to have him checked out by a specialist.

Helene called me at work, nearly crying. Of course, we were not hearing that our child was terminally sick, or had a lifetime of physical or mental struggle in front of him—parents who get that kind of news, and I've known a few, get up every morning to face the unspeakable, and I don't know how they do it; they are surely stronger than I'll ever be. No, our problem was one that we knew could be overcome with a little work and a little love, but still, it was a problem, a real one, and it made us angry at ourselves.

Dean seemed so lively, so aware, that we never worried about the fact that he called trucks "uck"—we thought it was cute. I guess we should have worried that he used this word for milk, too. Or that limousine was lim-o-leen. Or that bus was "bah," or that he couldn't pronounce the letter "c" at the beginning of a word or that he gave his own name as "Nean" or "Neannie."

We didn't notice that other children were ahead. Part of it might have been that, with me watching Dean during the days before going to work while Helene worked at home, we spent so much time with him that we understood every word no matter how it sounded. A parent who worked all day at the office might have noticed it sooner: progress, or the lack of it, stands out after a little time apart. We told our parents and friends about Rianne's observation, and they agreed: they had been worried, too. This made us even angrier—why hadn't they said something?

I'm sure it made Rianne uncomfortable to tell us this, and I'm forever grateful that she did, but it was a little awkward that the first person who told us our child was not 100 percent perfect, was not well ahead of the game, was an ex-girlfriend of mine, even though high school was fifteen years in the past. The night after we got the news I detected an unmistakable hint of tension in the air as Helene and I lay in bed; if I could just drift off, I thought, I'll be fine. But the more I thought about it, the more awake I became. The tension seemed to be coming from the other side of the mattress. I felt it rising. I gave up on sleep and tensed for whatever was coming.

"You know," Helene said, finally, "I don't need your ex-girlfriend telling me how to raise my child!"

The next day, not very rested, we got to work: we arranged for early-intervention counselors from the city to come interview us and evaluate Dean. I took him to an ear specialist, where he sat alone in a soundproof booth to have his hearing checked, raising his finger with each low tone.

Three young women soon crowded into our apartment. They interviewed us first, asking about Helene's pregnancy, about Dean's first steps. They paused while we described the day the World Trade Center came down.

I'd accidentally let Dean see the whole thing. We went to our window with its view of the harbor and downtown Manhattan after the first plane hit, and as I ran around and got dressed to go to work, he and his mother watched the endless smoke plume grow, and the ticker-tape parade of paper that swirled past our window, mixing in the breeze with the wails of a thousand sirens. I'd wondered as a child what would happen if a plane hit the buildings, but I'd never imagined two. When the second one roared out of the sky, in front of all of our eyes, I pulled my hair with both hands and shouted, "Holy shit!"

Dean imitated me doing this for days, although the words he used were indecipherable.

The counselors listened hard. "That might have something to do with it," one of them said.

Then they sat down with Dean. They asked him to stack some blocks (he got to eleven—the best they'd seen) and say all the words he knew. Here he didn't do so well. As they left, they explained that for the city to give Dean speech therapy, free, they'd have to make a determination that he was 33 percent behind where he was supposed to be. They offered to exaggerate his condition to get us the help, and we thanked them. But now I think they were just being nice when they said that: Dean was clearly 33 percent behind.

The report that came in the mail a few weeks later was filled with graphs and charts and written evaluations, all of which praised us as parents while complimenting the "nurturing" environment in the apartment, and said Dean was clearly able to understand everything being said to him. But in their conclusion, the Kind Speech Witches agreed that he needed help. They recommended speech therapy three times a week.

I couldn't help but feel that all the stuff about us being good, nurturing parents was added at the last minute as a consolation, to soften the blow.

Help soon arrived in the form of Elizabeth, a young therapist who was not herself a parent. Low-key, even dull, she tried to engage Dean but he didn't want anything to do with her. He was a different boy from the one he'd been when the evaluators were here, when he smiled and laughed, stacked those blocks and tried, really tried, to talk. Now he just wanted to go into his room.

Elizabeth grew annoyed, finally lecturing Helene that when a mother said no to her child, she had to mean no. Maybe she was right, but giving parenting tips wasn't why she was coming into our apartment, and she was promptly fired, joining the carcasses of Dr. Deutsch (*"Oh, let him cry!"*) and Olga the fortnightly cleaning lady (*"Your breast milk is no good!"*) on the smoldering ash heap of dismissed child-rearing and home-care specialists whose own words did them in.

It took the city a while to send a replacement, but when it did, all the crimes of honesty and omission committed by Rianne, Elizabeth and our friends and family were forgotten.

Corinne, a mother of three, was filled with energy and didn't care what made Dean talk as long as he did. M&M's, Hershey's Kisses—whatever was needed was offered. She lit up his bedroom like a bright light. She used a lollipop to show him where his tongue should touch his teeth, an effective method even if it eventually led to minor dental problems. She zipped through the neighborhood on her bicycle and was always in a rush, rarely staying more than fifteen minutes. But she never left without a hint of progress, and Dean loved her so, and wanted to impress her so, and wanted more chocolate so, that he gave it his best.

Corinne would close the door to his room; they'd work in private. Helene and I would sit in the living room, nervously, and practically swap high-fives when we heard her shriek and clap with delight—obviously, Dean had just gotten something right.

She told us what she was doing, and what the problem was. Dean had picked up some bad habits with the way he played his tongue against the top or bottom of his mouth, or behind his upper or lower teeth. I tested all of this myself in front of a mirror, seeing that speech is actually quite complicated if you break it into separate parts. She reassured us that Dean had plenty of intelligent thoughts in his head, it was just his ability to put them into words, and the creation of those words themselves, that needed work.

She told us we had done nothing wrong.

Dean ceased being Nean and started being Dean. Then "truck" and "bus" and "milk" came along, and "roro" became "water." Corinne was as thrilled as we were.

"You are my miracle child," she'd say to him as she strapped on her helmet and walked her bicycle to the elevator. Dean would push the button. Then we'd watch her from the window, rocketing down the street beneath pear trees just starting to bloom white and thicken with the coming spring.

By the time that fall when Dean started nursery school—where we saw, on the first day, girls de-coating the helpless boys—he was pretty damn understandable.

We weren't completely done: Corinne stayed with us for the rest of the year, and then said it was up to us, we could either quit with the therapy or have the city reevaluate him. We quit—we didn't see the need to have him checked out all over again. But it was a mistake: we had to pick up speech therapy two years later when his pronunciation problems had a brief relapse.

To me, the speech problems, and the relatively simple solution to them, exemplified this endless struggle in my head, of my desire not to compare my children to others, as hard as it can be. If I'd paid attention to the other children, then I might have heard that Dean wasn't speaking clearly.

But the biggest moral of all—besides the fact that it's not a bad idea to stay on good terms with the pretty girls you dated in high school—is that these problems come up when you are a parent, and it's nothing to be crushed by or to blame yourself about. I've been doing this fatherhood thing for only seven years, but one thing I've learned is that things seem to even out with a little time.

Think of all these comparisons—weight, walking, speech, writing, head circumference, toilet training, knowledge of the planets—and then take a ride on the subway or go to the mall and look at the crowds of people. They were all infants once. Now how many of them are wearing diapers, have unlaced shoes, can only crawl, are sobbing uncontrollably, are speaking incoherently, don't know the alphabet, don't know what Venus is, flip their coats up in the air, have giant heads and weigh 12.5 pounds?

Probably only a few.

Dean was sad when Corinne stopped coming by. "Where's my friend?" he'd ask, almost clearly. And when he said this, I realized she'd given us an even bigger gift than we'd realized. Because now that he could talk, he could do more than just describe what he saw or let us know what he wanted to eat or drink. He was three, and he'd been looking around for a while, unable to express himself. He'd seen a lot of things since getting here, and now he wanted explanations.

And so the questions began.

"What does 'from the horse's mouth' mean?"

—DEAN

James Lipton, host of *Inside the Actors Studio,* author of *An Exaltation of Larks* (Penguin, 1993; reprint edition), which traces the history and meaning of certain English expressions, and an experienced horseman:

> "'From the horse's mouth' is a bettor's term. It has to do with horse racing, because people always want to know everything they can before they put their money on the horse. And 'from the horse's mouth' means, quite simply, that somebody has inside information, and as close as you can get to the source

is the horse's mouth. In other words, the horse himself has confided in you. I don't think it's the least bit metaphorical, it's just a plain horseman's way of saying, 'I know this for a fact and this is the real McCoy.' There is one caveat: anybody who has spent a lot of time around horses knows they are singularly uncommunicative animals. They are not very talkative, unless they are Mr. Ed."

"Why do doctors have very messy writing?"

—ELLIOT APPLEBAUM, age six, La Jolla, California, after receiving a gift from his uncle, a doctor, accompanied by a note that no one in the family could read

Richard Orsini, forensic document examiner and handwriting expert, Jacksonville Beach, Florida:

"One word: impatience. They do not like having to write and sign lots and lots of documents during the day; they'd rather spend the time treating their patients. That's why a lot of the time their impatience shows in their handwriting; that's why they write illegibly, with lots of speed, because they want to get it over with. Sometimes you actually find doctors taking classes on how to write more legibly. It will come back to bite them if a pharmacist has a hard time interpreting their writing and gives the wrong medicine for a prescription, which has happened before. I had a case where a doctor was contending that a letter in a pharmacy prescription was an 'e' versus an 'i.' I said it was an 'i' and I showed an 'i' dot above it. It made a difference between someone taking a medicine four times a day versus once every four days. So that's what happened, and the individual lost his leg."

"What is the difference between joking and lying?"

—ARENAL GERSON HAUT, age four, Baltimore, Maryland

Jack Trimarco, expert forensic psychophysiologist, who ran the FBI polygraph (lie detection) unit at the Los Angeles field office from 1990 until 1998:

"A joke is aimed at making people laugh, and a lie is a self-serving misrepresentation whose purpose is to get out of trouble or minimize the seriousness of a situation."

ME: *"I guess people don't joke too much when you strap them in."*

"Sometimes they do, but it is a nervous reaction, such as 'Boy, I feel like I'm in the electric chair.' Well, that's not a good sign: they are supposed to see the polygraph as a savior that is going to get to the truth, and not as the executioner that is going to get to the truth."

"How does a joke register on the chart?"

"To understand how a polygraph works: there are only 'yes' and 'no' answers—'Did you rob the Bank of America?' Everything that you ask them is going to be reviewed with them beforehand, it won't be a surprise, and there is no room for humor once the test begins. If they want to joke about it, well, that's okay, but once the chart paper is rolling the only thing that they are going to say to me is 'yes' or 'no' to the previously reviewed questions."

"Let's say a person is born deaf and uses sign language and reads lips. When they think, do they think in words or in signs?"

—HANNAH BACHER, age nine, Baton Rouge, Louisiana

Beth S. Benedict, Ph.D., a faculty member at Gallaudet University, Washington, D.C., who was born deaf:

"It depends. If I think about things that are concrete, then I think in objects. If I think about people having a conversation, I see them signing—unless that person is hearing, then I see that person moving lips. If I think about things that are abstract, I see them in words."

"Who decides to name things? Like spoon, table, pencil, chair?"

—AVA GOLDEN, age five, Brooklyn, New York

Linda Picard Wood, senior editor, Merriam-Webster, Inc., Springfield, Massachusetts:

"People do. But no one knows for sure who first uttered the word 'spoon' or 'table.' Long ago, when people were trying to find ways to communicate, they put together sounds to form words. Eventually everyone in the group would come to use and understand a word to mean the same thing. This might happen in your own family. For example, in my family we sometimes use 'shake cheese' for grated Parmesan cheese (because you shake it out of the container). Each of us knows what we mean by 'shake cheese,' but no one really 'decided' that 'shake cheese' should be used for Parmesan cheese. It just happened over time.

"Words can change slowly. The word people used to mean 'spoon' a long time ago sounded a little different from our word 'spoon' today. Some words change a lot. And many words are taken from one language and used in another language, often a little differently. For example, our word 'table' goes way back to the word 'tabula' from Latin.

"Once in a while it does happen that a particular person gives something a name. For example, there's a number called a 'googol' that is a one with a hundred zeros after it. It was named a 'googol' by a little boy whose uncle was a mathematician who was working on math problems that involved the number. He asked his nephew what name to use for it, and his nephew told him to call it a 'googol.'"

"Why are Democrats donkeys and Republicans elephants?"

—ALEKS SIEMASZKO, age eight, Montclair, New Jersey

United States Senator Robert C. Byrd, D-West Virginia:

"The history of the donkey and elephant as the symbols of the Democratic and Republican parties goes back quite a long ways. The first time that the donkey was used in a political campaign for a Democratic candidate was in 1828, when Andrew Jackson used it on his campaign posters. During President Jackson's administration, the donkey represented the president's steadfast focus (some would say steadfast stubbornness). That donkey made its first appearance in a newspaper cartoon in 1837, and the symbol has stayed with the Democratic Party ever since.

"As for the Republican Party's symbol of the elephant, it was another cartoonist, Thomas Nast, who penned a cartoon in 1874 that really cemented the link between the party and the pachyderm. In that cartoon, Nast showed an elephant representing Republican voters supporting a possible third term for President Ulysses Grant. The link was formed, and the elephant continues to represent the Republican Party to this day.

"Interestingly, while the Republican Party has officially adopted the elephant as its party symbol, the Democratic Party has never officially done the same with the humble donkey, though the image has been used for more than a century in various party designs and publications."

"How did the pineapple get its name?"

—SYDNEY DURDEN, age five, Menlo Park, California

Dan Nellis, operations director, Dole Food Company Hawaii, Wahiawa, Oahu:

"On one of Christopher Columbus's voyages to America, to the Caribbean Sea area, to some of the islands, his sailors came upon an empty village of the Carib Indians and there was fruit piled up on the ground that had been picked, and they took it and sampled it. And it resembled the pinecone and had a sweet taste and crunchy texture like an apple, and that's where the name came from. Of course it was in

Spanish, so I don't know how it translated into English. *Pina* is what they call it in Spanish because it has the resemblance to the pinecone. It is a native fruit to South America and the Caribbean islands; it is not native to Hawaii, it was brought to Hawaii. Originally, Spanish sailors had it with them."

"What is Tiki?"

—WILL POPALISKY, age six, Brooklyn, New York

Mike Buhan, who owns Tiki-Ti in Los Angeles and whose father, Ray Buhan, worked in the 1930s with Don "the Beachcomber" Gantt, generally acknowledged as the father of Tiki cocktail culture:

"Tiki is a lot of things. It comes from Polynesian cultures where there are all kinds of carvings, called tikis, of various gods—the God of Love, the God of War. Tiki style began in the 1930s; that's when my dad worked with Don the Beachcomber in the original bar that he opened on McCadden Place in Hollywood right after Prohibition ended. He was one of four Filipinos who actually worked there when it opened up. Don got all this tropical stuff together and rented out this tiny place and opened up a little bar, and all of the movie industry people started hanging out there, and that was the start of the Tiki craze. It really took off right after World War II because a lot of the GIs were in the South Pacific, and when they came back they were already accustomed to the islands, the tropical stuff. That's why it kind of flourished. Basically, Tiki is escapism: you're in a big city and you open a door and you step into another world."

"Why is noon p.m. instead of a.m., since it has been a.m. right up to twelve o'clock?"

—DREW RICKARD, age eleven, Burlington, Vermont

Demetrios Matsakis, Ph.D., head of the Time Service Department, United States Naval Observatory, Washington, D.C.:

"People raised in different cultures often do things very differently, often because that's how they learned from the previous generation. In Japan, they started saying that noon was twelve a.m., and that's how they think of it. And they call midnight either zero a.m. or twelve p.m. They're not any more wrong or any more correct than we are. Actually we are both wrong, and we should not say that noon and midnight are either 'a.m.' or 'p.m.' They are simply noon and midnight.

"The terms 'a.m.' and 'p.m.' came to us almost by accident. Long ago, Greek and Roman astronomers conceived of the meridian—an imaginary line in the sky that goes from north to south. It goes from the most northerly spot on the horizon through Polaris, the North Star. Then it goes straight overhead, and continues on down towards the south. In the mornings, the sun is rising towards the meridian. So the Romans used the term *ante meridiem,* which is Latin for 'before meridian.' The abbreviation is 'a.m.' Exactly at noon the sun is on the meridian. Then in the afternoon the sun has passed the meridian and is going down, and so they called it *post meridiem,* or 'p.m.' Almost no one speaks Latin anymore, but we still say 'a.m.' and 'p.m.'"

"Why is it called 'kidnapping' if you can steal away adults, too?"

—ALEX AGUILERA, age nine, Clifton, Virginia

John F. Fox, Jr., official historian of the FBI, Washington, D.C.:

"The word 'kidnap' brings together the words 'kid' (originally slang when applied to people) and 'nap/nab,' meaning 'to take.' The combination of the two words appears in the late seventeenth century and referred to the taking of youths for slave labor. Likely the first use of the word was as a noun referring to people who engaged in taking slaves, kidnappers, and eventually became a verb, 'to kidnap.' As slavers took able-bodied adults as well, the use of the term came to describe all who engaged in this practice. By the mid-1700s, the English legal theorist Blackstone noted that the official definition of 'kidnapping' entailed the forcible abduction of a man, woman or child. Thus, in less than seventy years, kidnapping has come to mean the taking of any person."

"Why do they call it soccer? They don't play in socks."

—OLIVIA FOLEY, age six, Fairfield, Connecticut, while watching English Premier League highlights with her father

Sunil Gulati, President, U.S. Soccer Federation:

"Well, most players actually do play in socks, they just also wear shoes over their socks. But that's not why they call it soccer. The real reason is that in England, where the sport became organized for the first time nearly 150 years ago, they called it 'football.' However, another sport was also becoming known as football: rugby, which became the football we know here in the United States. So to differentiate between these two footballs they started calling rugby 'rugby football' and soccer 'association football,' because of the organized association (in England) playing football. From there, the word 'association' was shortened to 'assoc' or 'soc,' which became 'soccer' and was used as a slang term for football. That is the word that eventually moved to the United States to describe the game."

"What is legal and what is illegal?"

—JUDE RIZZO, age three, New York City

Justice Barbara J. Pariente, Florida Supreme Court:

"What is 'legal' is based on rules that everyone must follow. Rules—or laws—allow us to get along with one another. If a person does not follow the rules, that person acts in a way that is illegal. For example, it is illegal or against the rules to hit someone else. But rules must be fair to everyone and treat everyone equally. So if it was legal to hit someone if they had blue eyes or it was only illegal to hit someone if they had brown eyes, that would not be fair. Many years ago there were laws that made black people sit in the back of buses. In some states, that was 'legal' but it was not fair. Judges make sure that the laws are fair to everyone based on the Constitution of the United States. Judges and juries also decide if the person has followed the law or has broken the law.

"Imagine a planet where there were no rules for anything, not even for games, and what the consequences would be. Think about what a game of baseball would be like on this planet. You would not even be able to play baseball because there would be no rules to tell you how to do it. It works the same between people. When people follow the rules and act in a 'legal' way, it is much easier to get along."

"What is the Q in Q-tip for?"

—SOPHIE INDIANA BAKER, age six, Brooklyn, New York

Stacie Bright, Unilever senior communications marketing manager, Q-tips:

"In 1923, Leo Gerstenzang, original founder of the Q-tips Company, conceived the idea of Q-tips cotton swabs after observing his wife apply wads of cotton to toothpicks for their daughter's daily bath. The product was originally named Baby Gays after Gerstenzang's baby Gayle. It wasn't until 1926 that the name was changed to Q-tips Baby Gays. Later the Baby Gays mark was discarded and the product name shortened to Q-tips. The Q in the name Q-tips stands for 'quality' and the word 'tips' describes the cotton swabs on the end of the stick."

I'm not the first parent to remember his child's questions. Some of the best ones we never forget. And our children remember asking. My friend Gia in New Brunswick asked a great one when she was little. In her training as a psychologist, which was quite lengthy, she came across the answer to the question she had asked thirty years earlier.

"How come if you forget what you were going to say, you don't forget that you were going to say something?"

—GIANINE ROSENBLUM, age nine, Brooklyn, New York

Gianine Rosenblum, Ph.D., age thirty-nine, licensed psychologist, therapist and child development researcher:

> "The reason is that there is more than one type of memory, and as far as I understand it, the part of your memory that holds the desire to make a comment is your working memory, which keeps stuff at hand and is very active. If there is something you want to share, an idea or a memory, it is in long-term storage. You have to get from your working memory to your long-term storage, and sometimes you get interrupted. It's like you are in a truck and you are on your way to long-term storage, but you get run off the road; the thread is broken. You know you are in the truck—in other words, you know you want to make a comment—but because something or someone interrupted you, you have forgotten where you are going."

7.

Tough Ones

When she was little, Helene's friend Kathy asked the same question again and again, posing it to her mother and, during confessional, to her priest. It's a question every parent has heard, with a million variations: Where do babies come from? Finally her mother, doubtless harried and in a terrible rush, wrestling with the query for the hundredth time, had had enough. She knew she had to give an answer, any answer. Here is what she said:

"At the Woolworth's on Central Avenue."

From that moment on, every time little Kathy and her mother walked past the store, she would see all the women with boys and girls and babies sitting in the shopping carts, and be certain that a sale was going on, a sale on small children. She would beg her mother, again and again, to go in and buy one. Maybe they were even free.

Fibbing to your children, even for good reasons, can have unintended consequences.

Helene created an elaborate back story to explain Dean's arrival to him. He was in heaven, she said, floating around and around, gently somersaulting through the clouds, looking for a mommy and daddy to live with. When he picked us, someone—God? A doctor?—placed Dean in her belly, where he cooked for a while until he was ready to come out.

I liked the idea of little Dean floating through the clouds. He did, too: "I was looking for a pretty mommy named Helene and a daddy named Wendell who worked at a newspaper—and then I found you," he'd tell us. But as he got older, he came to realize that there were some parts of this story that did not quite add up.

We were sitting one evening on the screened-in porch of the little cottage in the country when he asked: "So after the baby gets put inside the mommy's belly, how does it get out?"

Helene glanced at me. A moth fluttered outside the screen and a heron glided above the smooth orange surface of the tidal estuary. Dean was five. I thought about it and I decided he could take the truth. I gave Helene a look that said: *Lay it on him.*

"Well," she said, tentatively, "the baby comes out of the mommy's poochie."

The poochie pseudonym comes from Helene's family and has always been funny to me, because my family has a very old and dear friend who goes by the same name. But there was no time for thoughts of her now; Dean was mulling. He scrunched up his face. "But then the baby would only be this big," he said, holding his fingers about a half-inch apart.

It had been two years since Paulina was born, in the same

ward at New York Hospital as Dean. He had first seen her when she was twelve hours old, expressionless, a thick shock of black hair on her head just like when her brother was born. He held her and said, "We have a big family now," as I stood nearby, proud but ready to dive for the catch if he dropped her. He therefore knew, firsthand, that a baby isn't two inches long when it is born, the size he presumed a poochie to be.

I said: "Well, that part of mommy kind of, um, expands."

Dean nodded his head to the side, and then looked away: he had already tired of the poochie-newborn spatial relations conundrum; he'd moved on to the next pressing matter in his head. Helene and I relaxed. His eyes focused in the middle distance, on a dark clump of trees set in the reeds across the water. He then asked his follow-up question:

"Do vampire bats live in Pennsylvania?"

That first one, "Where do babies come from?" is a true perennial, a question that has bedeviled parents, I'm sure, since humans first learned to communicate. One mother said Woolworth's, we said clouds. Dean still has not asked exactly what I had to do with him and his sister being born; that part of the process would surely shock him. We tried to be honest, but our honesty mixed with the gentle fibs we'd kept going for years. The result was that Dean simply tuned us out and moved on to the next thing.

But it was only one of a million tricky questions. And in many ways, the easiest of them: it's grown-ups who've made birth and everything leading up to it weird-sounding and complicated. But how do we answer the really tough questions? How do we explain a world where nations hurl missiles at each other, and entire races have been forced into slavery, and women have been denied fair chances because they are women? How do we answer questions about torture, and drug abuse, and cruelty?

What do we say when entire buildings, the tallest in sight, collapse in flames outside our living room windows?

We do our best, that's all.

"Where do babies come from?" is a snap compared with those.

If birth is the beginning and prompts tough questions, questions about the end are even harder. How do you explain the unexplainable?

Nicholas Hurley, age three, the son of a friend, was sitting on his kitchen counter watching his mother, Vicky, make dinner when he asked her: "What is die?" and "Do I want to die?"

Vicky paused, put down the salad bowl and explained that he probably didn't want to die quite yet.

"Why?"

Because, she said, she wanted him to be with her for many more years and wanted to watch him grow up. And didn't he want to live a long time, to reach old age? She got surprisingly emotional. Nicholas sensed this and decided to have some fun, saying over and over again that he wanted to die, nearly causing Vicky to burst into tears.

But her older daughter, Nell, who was six, was an even tougher proposition.

"When are *you* going to die?" she asked. Having practiced this sort of thing on her younger son, Vicky was ready. She explained that she didn't know, really, but she hoped it would be many years in the future, and pointed out that both her parents were still alive. She said she would be around to watch her daughter graduate from school, get a job, get married and have her own children—just as her own parents had been around to see her do all these things.

But she had taken the analogy too far. Her daughter looked at her. Now she began to cry.

"But then you'll be an old lady and I don't want an old lady for a mother."

My friend Greg's son Damon was four, watching a show about mummies, when one of his cousins told him: "That's what you are going to look like when you die." Damon had never considered his own mortality, and became alarmed. He started sobbing.

Greg sat Damon down and asked him how old he was. He asked him to count to eighty-six, which he did. I'm not sure why Greg picked eighty-six as the magical death age—the current life expectancy for an American male born now is seventy-five—but his gambit worked: the sheer number of integers little Damon had had to enumerate between four and eighty-six proved that death was not something he had to worry about just then.

With Dean, and I'm sure with most children, the ever-soothing concept of heaven proves helpful when confronting death queries. That's where you go when you die, and it's a great place—fluffy clouds, lots of trucks, pretty girls. In one of his kinder moments Dean said: "Daddy, if you are going to heaven, I'm going to grab your leg and you can pull me up with you."

"Dino," I told him, "do me a favor: grab me and pull me back down instead."

Helene mumbled something under her breath. Dean couldn't hear it but I could.

It was: "I'm not sure your father is going to heaven."

Are we lying when we talk about heaven to our children? We lie about Santa Claus, and sometimes other questions for which we don't know the answers. We lie about Woolworth's. The heaven lie, to me, is the most worthwhile. When we are adults, we still can't get our arms around death—how can a child?

So that's one approach. But I really think Greg had the right idea: put some distance between the kid and the great beyond. Dean has never asked, straightaway, when or how or why he might die; perhaps he senses that the honest answer to this question is something of a downer. But he has asked things that hint around the edges, like, "When I'm fifty, how old will you be?" (Eighty-three.) "Will you be dead?"

While the answer, most likely, is yes, unless I begin some type of strenuous health regime that is in direct contrast to the way I've taken care of myself for the last forty years, I hedge my bets a bit here like Vicky and Greg and point out to him that there are two generations in our family who must confront death before me, and three before him, as long as we look both ways when we cross the street and don't smoke or drink too much.

My parents are both alive, and my stepparents and even one of my grandparents, my mother's father, known to me and my sister and our cousins from North Carolina as Pop Pop. Dean has met him many times. He was a superior court judge in Pennsylvania (where there are no vampire bats); my mother took Lindsay and me to see him up on the bench in his black robes when we were little. He was hearing the appeal of a man who had set his girlfriend's door on fire because she wouldn't have his baby.

"Pop Pop is very old," Dean said, accurately.

Yes, Pop Pop was born in 1910, when horses walked down the cobblestone street outside our apartment, when only a few airplanes had ever flown—and those that did were made of sticks and canvas—when sailing ships were still regularly seen in New York Harbor, when there was no radio, no television and certainly no cell phones or Internet. See how much changed since Pop Pop was a boy? Imagine, I tell him, how the world will look when you are old—flying cars, space travel, whatever. It is so far in the future it is almost impossible to imagine. But when Dean tries, my mission is accomplished. The issue of death is temporarily forgotten, or placed in an unimaginable future, to be asked about another day.

I know I asked my parents a few tough questions. I asked about testicles when a torture victim on television said electrodes had been attached to his. I worried about nuclear war, like probably every other kid who grew up between the 1950s and 1970s. Walter Cronkite talked about how many times the United States or the Soviet Union could obliterate the planet with their missiles. It seemed like overkill to me, destroying the planet more than once; I asked my dad what was stopping either one of us from just firing our ICBMs.

"Wen, imagine if you had a fish bowl and a brick," he said, starting an explanation that I imagine he had practiced or heard somewhere, it was so thoroughly thought out. "And imagine your friend had a fish tank and a brick. Well, if you smashed his fish tank, he would just smash yours. So what would be the point?"

My best friend at this age was a kid named Elliot Bertoni. He was blond and had freckles. The idea of him smashing my fish tank with a brick—which I now saw in my mind, complete with water spraying, flying shards of glass and doomed fish flapping around on the floor—seemed as absurd as the idea of one country winning a war by destroying the planet.

I asked another dicey one around this time: "What's wrong with Louis's dad?"

This was at the end of the birthday party where we fired off rockets in the park. After the cake, the other boys' parents started arriving to pick them up. After a while, only my friend

Louis was left. For half an hour, as the air cooled as it does on late May evenings, the two of us played in the backyard.

Then his father showed up, a middle-aged man in a green raincoat and a crumpled black hat. He was smoking a cigarette. But what was most distinctive about him was the way he was walking, kind of weaving around, pausing at awkward moments and laughing a little too hard at everything my father said. Louis seemed annoyed and rushed his dad out of the house. I experienced a vague cringing sensation I had never felt before. After my father locked the gate and came back into the hallway, I asked him what was wrong.

"Oh, Wen, sometimes people go out to celebrate, have a good time, and they celebrate a little too much and they have a little too much to drink. I think Louis's dad just maybe celebrated too much this afternoon."

This made me happy for him, that he'd been able to have a nice celebration at the same time as my party.

I asked my parents about nuclear war and about a friend's drunken father, but I never asked them about the war in our house.

The fights began soon after we moved to Brooklyn, in the evenings, after Lindsay and I had been put to bed in our room on the third floor. Indistinct voices at first, raised just slightly, then shouts, then out-and-out screams punctuated by smashing glass, and even, once, the reflected flashing red-and-white lights of a police radio car that had been called by neighbors.

Anything could set off these fights.

One Saturday night we were watching *Adam-12* in the kitchen while we ate dinner. I liked these two clean-cut policemen driving under blue skies, lawns everywhere; they looked a lot different from the cops who had come to our house. I asked my dad if he liked these two California policemen, too.

"No," he said. He sort of rolled his eyes and his head at the same time. "They're a couple of ignorant clods."

My mother glared at him. "Jamie, I'm not sure you should call police officers 'ignorant clods' in front of the children. And how do you know they're 'ignorant clods' anyway? Have you met them? They seem nice enough to me."

My dad rolled his eyes again, even exaggerating the gesture a little. He seemed to enjoy getting this reaction.

"Oh, of course they're ignorant clods, look at them."

"Jamie!"

"Well, they are."

Lindsay and I glanced at each other.

After we were in bed, the shouting began.

I also remember tension about some kind of drill my father bought for my mother. That's not as bad as it sounds—my mother was now several years into her career as a goldsmith—but something about the drill was not quite right. This prompted a dirty look from her after she opened it, and dirty looks in return, and again the issue simmered all day before boiling over after bedtime.

I'd try to fall asleep before I heard the first distant voices. But then as now, trying to fall asleep kept me awake. *("Ronan puts on his coat the regular way," my sister would say one day.)* I'd listen closely, hoping that the first high-pitched squawks were fragments of laughter and not angry screams. Lindsay and I would then sit on the carpeted steps, leaning on the creaking dark wood balustrade, trying to pick out enough words between the slamming of doors and cupboards to figure out what was going on. We'd construct a cohesive narrative. The sounds were muffled, but the rage seeped through those heavy doors.

The house had very old light switches, three round buttons on each floor landing that turned off the hallway lights on the floor you were on, as well as the one below and the one above. Lindsay and I would press them, turning the lights on and off on the other floors, trying to get our parents' attention. Finally, we would go downstairs, bleary-eyed, and the sight of us in our footie pajamas and nightgown would usually deflate the conflagration, at least for the night.

Once the fight erupted on a Saturday afternoon and came up to the bedrooms: it moved like a thunderstorm from the front of the house to the back; one of the glass panels in the doors between our room and our parents' room was kicked out, shattering into a hundred pieces.

This went on for years.

One by one, my friends' parents got divorced, beginning with Elliot Bertoni's. Soon it seemed that every family in Park Slope had separated. I have a theory that the beauty in those houses, all the woodwork and antique beveled mirrors and raised details in the plaster, helped drive families apart. It was as though the reality of being married and having children could never live up to the ideal of a happy home carved into those details; the houses mocked the stressed families living in them and set a standard of perfection that could never be attained by humans.

When my parents told me and my sister that they, too, were splitting, the four of us sitting around the kitchen table, there were tears, but not as many as might have been expected. I felt a mix of emotions—abject terror at the huge change about to descend on our house, with my dad gone, but also, quite clearly in my memory, relief.

This was a few days after Christmas, the Christmas when my sister put her tooth under the pillow and it was still there when she woke up, the Christmas Santa Claus ran over the tooth fairy with his sleigh. My parents had decided to split a few months earlier, but wanted to wait until after the holidays to tell us. During this time, this Phony War in our house, there had been no fights, no slammed doors, no police. There was even laughter from my mother as my father joked about the tooth fairy that morning. Lindsay and I had wondered what was going on, hopeful yet hesitant—I hesitated to ask what was going on because I didn't want to spoil it.

When they told us Dad was moving out, I felt the same as I had in woodworking class a few years before when a couple of rotten boys told me gleefully that there was no Santa Claus: it made obvious, yet tragic, sense.

I swore to myself that Helene and I would never fight in front of Dean, or even let the sounds of anger reach his ears. Listening to my parents fight were the most awful moments of a childhood that was otherwise filled with funny answers, and happy summers, and a beautiful home, and good music.

I kept my promise until I broke it.

A fight can come out of the relaxed air of a Saturday morning like a summer squall: you can't see it on the horizon, it doesn't show up on radar. A few words are exchanged and the situation is suddenly untenable—nations release their missiles, enough to destroy the planet a dozen times over, and there is no stopping them once they leave the silos.

That Saturday morning was dragging on. Paulina was crying, the neighbors downstairs complaining as Dean ran across their ceiling. Neither Helene nor I had had a good night's sleep. I decided to take Dean to the amusement park at Coney Island to spend a few hours on the kiddie rides, and called a friend to see if he and his son wanted to come along. He liked the idea of Coney Island and we made a plan.

But after we were all dressed and ready to go, he called back and said that he'd be about two hours late. Dean and I went into standby mode. His sneakers came off and he ran around some more. The baby cried. The neighbors banged. The apartment, spacious by Brooklyn standards, got very small.

I snapped at Dean, and Helene glared at me.

"He's allowed to run around his own apartment," she said. "Why don't you guys just go early and wait."

I put my shoes back on and got Dean's sneakers. I slipped them on his feet and started to tie the laces when I felt Helene's presence over my shoulder. I looked up at her.

"Be sure to double knot them," she said.

"Yes, I know how to tie shoelaces."

"I'm not sure you do."

"I know how to tie shoelaces."

"Barely."

(My mother: "They seem nice enough to me.")

(My father: "Oh, of course they're ignorant clods, look at them.")

Dean and I put on our coats and headed out the door. But I was angry about Helene's tone of voice, the way she had questioned my shoe-tying ability, and I decided to call her on my cell phone and tell her so. I fumbled with it with one hand while holding Dean's in the other as we walked down the street. But this was bad timing.

"I'm just picking up your socks," she said as she answered, before I even got started, echoing a complaint about my own personal laundry disposal that my mother could have made thirty years earlier. "Do you have to be such a pig?"

Now the cell phone wasn't good enough: I had to go back

and yell at Helene in person. I told her I was going to do this and hung up. Dean and I retraced our steps, back through the lobby and into the elevator. My heart pounded. I felt myself get angrier and angrier as the floor numbers on the elevator lit up one by one. I work hard all week, I thought—*I can leave my socks around!*

The front door of our apartment was shut. I got out my keys and undid the locks, but the door would only give a few inches: Helene had locked the chain. I pushed a few times but it wouldn't go. I yelled through the six-inch crack, the chain taut against the bridge of my nose, sort of like Jack Nicholson in *The Shining*, except instead of "Here's Johnny" I was saying: "I am not a pig!" and "I can leave my socks around!" and "I know how to tie shoes!"

I had always wondered about that chain. How strong was it, really? It seemed pretty crappy. If a gang of kidnappers wanted to take my wife and children, and pillage and destroy my apartment, would it stop them? I tested it now by throwing the weight of my body against the door. The chain snapped without the meekest complaint, and I was suddenly in the apartment, a little surprised, and Helene was fuming at me, even more surprised. Dean seemed impressed that I had broken through so easily.

Helene and I started yelling at each other from two feet away. She even went into a fighting stance—left fist raised, right fist cocked. I was ready to take her on when Dean let out a high-pitched scream from the threshold. It practically shook the apartment and shattered the windows; I wouldn't have been surprised had it been heard in Manhattan. It even quieted Paulina down. We turned to look at him.

"Stop it!" he said.

And we did.

You could almost feel the air rushing out of the room.

Dean had screamed the way Lindsay and I had pushed on ancient light switches and then descended groggily down creaking stairs in footie pajamas. His method was more direct, but the result was the same—the fight stopped, the clouds dissipated, the missiles went backward as the film rewound.

Later that night at bedtime, memories of a delayed but still successful Coney Island outing fresh in his head, he asked me about it. "Why did you guys yell at each other?"

"Well, kid, you yell and scream sometimes. You yell at me. And Paulina, she screams all the time—"

"She's a baby."

"Okay, she is. Good point. What I'm saying is, people who love each other still get angry and yell at each other all the time. Mommy and I were just in a bad mood, that's all."

"You really broke that door down. You were like King Kong."

"I didn't break it down, Dean, I just broke the lock. It was like a test to see how strong it was. You know, when I was little my mother and father—Pops and Grandma Bessie—used to fight all the time. For a while it was every night. They broke lots of things. Lindsay and I used to sit on the stairs and listen for hours. The police even came once. Pops or Grandma Bessie, I forget which one, smashed a panel of glass in a door. It went all over the place."

"Wait—Pops and Grandma Bessie used to live together?"

"Yes, of course. They're my parents."

"What about Kathy and Tom?" (These are my stepparents.)

"It was before they met them, before they got divorced."

"What is divorced?"

"It's when two people who were married get unmarried." I thought to myself: *While almost all of my friends' parents split when I was little, I can think of only one of Dean's friends whose parents live apart.*

"Why did they fight all the time?"

"You know, I'm not sure. I don't think I ever asked them. I know they were much younger than your mother and I were when they got married and had kids. I think Grandma Bessie thought Pops was annoying, that he spent too much time telling her what to think, and I think Pops thought Grandma Bessie was angry too much of the time, had a bad temper. I think he actually enjoyed getting her angry sometimes. Also, it was the seventies—it was a different time, man."

"Well, if they were fighting all the time and I was little I would have told them to stop. I would have done what I did today: I would have yelled really loud, and they would have had to stop, or people would have come to the house."

"That would have been a good idea."

"Because today, you know, I saved the day."

"If the Empire State Building was hit by a plane, would it fall down, too?"

—DEAN, three years after 9/11

Ron Klemencic, structural engineer, former chairman of the Council on Tall Buildings and Urban Habitat, Illinois Institute of Technology, Chicago:

"The planes that hit the World Trade Center—the bombs, really—were huge and filled with fuel, as opposed to the plane that hit the Empire State Building in 1945, which was much smaller. Some of the photographs of the World Trade Center after the planes had hit—but before the buildings had collapsed—showed gaping holes; in one of them, you can actually see the imprint of the airplane that hit it. It is almost from wingtip to wingtip. And you can see the structure around that opening almost acting like a bridge, holding up the rest of the building. The floors of the World Trade Center were unusually large, so that when the planes hit they didn't slice the buildings in half. The planes may have sliced any other buildings in half. The speculation is that any other building would not have fared nearly as well, and that the devastation would have been much more immediate."

Engineers, I've learned, are as cautious with their opinions as they are with their buildings. And this question is so speculative that it seemed impossible that there was only one answer. So I went in search of a second opinion. I can only hope we never find out who's right.

Silvian Marcus, Cantor Seinuk Group, the engineer of record for both 7 World Trade Center (which collapsed on 9/11) and its replacement:

"The Empire State Building was hit by an airplane, a B-25 bomber, back in 1945. This was a light plane without the speed that planes have today, and it may not have had a large tank of gasoline, and there was no structural damage at all. The jets that hit the World Trade Center were much bigger and faster; the larger the plane and the higher the speed—the velocity—the larger the energy of the blow. It is like a hammer: the heavier the hammer, the more muscular the person swinging it, the faster the hammer goes.

"But there are major differences between the buildings. The methods and technology used at the time the Empire State Building was built were developed to a lesser degree than they are today; same with the mathematics and the physics. This meant engineers had the tendency of being very prudent, if not to say more conservative. So what is the difference? This building is a steel building, like the World Trade Center, but is done with many, many pieces, and many connections. There is this fabric of so many pieces interrelated—all the steel is covered with either brick or stone or concrete or other materials, both for aesthetics and fire protection. Today you see lots of glass and lots of metal, light materials. If jets hit the building at five hundred miles per hour, it would be seriously damaged, but my belief is that the building would not collapse, it would stand, because of the fabric of material. If one or more pieces of the fabric were destroyed, the others would take the weight, the suffering. It is like a very large family of people: the larger it is, the harder it is to destroy."

"Why do they put clothes on people who die? No one's gonna see them."

—ALYSSA WENDOLOWSKI, age seven, Springfield, New Jersey

Bill Bromirski, a fourth-generation owner of Bromirski Funeral Home, Jersey City, New Jersey, which has been in the same family since before 1896:

"Everybody who goes out of our funeral home is fully dressed, including underclothes, socks, shoes, all garments. Because my father always said that when we have the last accounting up in Heaven, he doesn't want anyone standing there in the nude. We dress everybody, whether someone is going to see the person or not. It is a custom with us. It is to show respect. Let me take it a step further: occasionally we will bury someone who doesn't have any family, and when we take the body into church, if there is no one there, we stay. We stay as the closest person to them—no one should go alone. These are just the customs that have evolved. Same thing with the clothing. We do Muslim funerals. There is a tradition that the body be wrapped in new cloth, brand-new muslin or linen, that is cut specifically to fit the body. There is a ritual prayer service, washing and dressing. That is a requirement. It can get traumatic if you are a young man or woman and you have to wash the body of your mother or father who died suddenly. That can be hard. But it is all out of respect."

"Why is there war?"

—CONRAD KASSIN, age four, Los Angeles, California, after watching his cousins play a particularly violent video game

Colonel John J. Smith, United States Military Academy at West Point, a twenty-five-year army veteran who commanded an artillery battery during the 1991 Gulf War:

"I've been thinking about this for a couple of decades. Some psychologists would say that humans—and especially men—are inherently violent; this comes from our evolution. Some sociologists would say that war and organized conflicts are necessary to building cohesion and a sense of identity within a culture. And we could debate those points, but I think it really comes down to four big reasons.

"The first one would be economics. Groups of people either have real, imagined or perceived differences or inequalities—somebody has more than I do. Maybe there really is a need, maybe a country has famines or drought and they are lacking basic resources, and a neighboring country has those resources, and if they can't obtain these peacefully, sometimes they are forced—or think they are forced—to go and get them.

"That would bring us to our second big reason for war: fear. We fear that people will come and take the things we have, we fear people will come and harm us or harm our families, and this can lead to preemptive wars: we would rather fight them on their home territory than let them fight here. Sometimes this fear leads us into coalitions or allegiances—and because we have an agreement with someone else, we are forced into a war.

"And that leads us to our third reason: our sense of honor. Honor means different things to different cultures over the centuries. Sometimes a sense of honor becomes a little bit overblown or escalated, and we get into wars of vengeance or retaliation. There may have been a good reason to go to war, maybe it began as a perceived just war or a justifiable war, but then it becomes a matter of retaliation over the years—we can point to the situations in the Middle East or Northern Ireland as examples of this.

"And that brings us to our fourth big reason for war: we have different ideologies, ways of thinking about religion or thinking about government. Some of these belief systems require expansion of this ideology. Some people thought

Fascism or Communism was the way to go, and wanted to force the whole world under that umbrella. We think one way of living is better than another, and we want to force others to our way of thinking. You can mix and match various degrees of all of those four reasons, really."

"What if a mom really wants a baby but can't have one?"

—FREYA ERIKSEN, age five, San Jose, California

Dr. Jerald S. Goldstein, reproductive endocrinologist, Dallas:

"I sit down with a couple and go through basically everything, all their options, all the stats associated with each treatment. And then it's up to them. It is done like a typical algorithm: the younger you are, the less invasive treatment you start off with, unless it is a clearly identifiable problem. You want to find out how far a couple wants to go in terms of treatment, how much time and how aggressive they want to be.

"The least invasive would be Clomid, which induces ovulation, with timed intercourse or intrauterine insemination. Typically, you try that for two or three months. After that, I might talk to women about injectable medications. This would be injectable medications with intrauterine insemination or in vitro fertilization. In vitro fertilization often represents the best option in terms of pregnancy rates, approximately sixty-five percent in women thirty-four and under; however, they decline with age. For older women, using an egg donor may need to be considered, which has a pregnancy rate of about eighty-five percent. That is the medical part; there is also the physical and emotional part of treatment which needs to be addressed. The cost of in vitro is typically around ten thousand dollars; however, with the use of an egg donor it increases to about eighteen thousand to twenty thousand dollars. Adoption is always an option, and we always try to help couples have an understanding of their options."

"Why did people have slaves?"

—REBECCA GUDZY, age six, Montclair, New Jersey

Gerald A. Foster, Ph.D., scholar-in-residence, United States National Slavery Museum, Fredericksburg, Virginia, a descendant of slaves who owns an 1846 slave coin that once belonged to his great-grandfather:

"Before the Civil War, approximately twenty-five percent to thirty percent of Americans owned slaves. They purchased and maintained them for the free labor they provided both in the North and South for more than two hundred years. Furthermore, after the American Revolution and the ratification of the U.S. Constitution, slaveholding became a very substantial element of political power and influence in the areas of taxation as well as proportional representation in the Congress (Three-Fifths Compromise).

"So why did people have slaves? Answer: primarily to amass wealth and to gain political power. Socially, slaves were rendered less than human and were objectified as property. Slave owners were therefore able to justify scientifically and religiously the inhumane and heinous treatment of their slaves. It was the beginning of the class-oriented structure of early America, which eventually evolved into late-nineteenth-century and early-twentieth-century prejudice, discrimination and racism directed almost exclusively at African Americans."

"Why are there no lady presidents?"

—JACK LANCASTER, age seven, Los Angeles, California

Pat Schroeder, former twelve-term congresswoman from Colorado, who was the first woman to serve on the House Armed Services Committee and who considered a run for the presidency in 1988:

"It's almost a catch-22: we haven't had any presidents who looked like women, so we can't envision one. Visuals are important. Countries in Europe and elsewhere have had queens and empresses and all kinds of women who ran them. We say 'Commander in Chief,' 'Leader of the Free World,' so we see a military/macho type of president, and it is very hard for women to fit that image. We have never had a woman secretary of defense, we haven't had a woman on the Joint Chiefs. Luckily, two women have been secretary of state, and that helps, but this military thing—'Commander in Chief,' 'Leader of the Free World'—has always made me nuts, because we have had all sorts of male presidents who have never served in the military and somehow it doesn't matter. I always say America is the ultimate tree house with a 'No Girls Allowed' sign on it. Look, we have a female helicopter pilot from Iraq running for Congress. We are beginning to see women work their way through the military, and while people aren't totally comfortable with it, they are much more comfortable with it than they were even ten years ago. We have had women who are the head of their class at West Point. Gradually it is seeping into the culture that women can manage security issues, but there has always been this view that women are too softhearted. I always remind people that in nature it is the lioness you don't want to run into, while the male lion is asleep somewhere."

"Is George Bush evil? Mommy said so."

—NATE CONRAD, age five, Rockaway, New Jersey

Malcolm David Eckel, Ph.D., director of the Institute for Philosophy and Religion at Boston University, which recently sponsored a multiyear investigation of the concept of evil in philosophy and religion:

"I can understand where your mother is coming from. The world seems to be getting more and more violent all the time, and anyone who seems to contribute to the violence, as we have been doing in Iraq, can seem to be evil. But 'evil' is a strong word.

"Immanuel Kant, one of the most influential philosophers who has written about evil, said that it is evil anytime someone decides to do something for selfish reasons without considering the interests of others. By this definition, just about everybody is evil at one time or another, including me, you, your mother, President Bush and anybody else you would care to name. Other people think that the word 'evil' should be reserved for only the most horrible crimes, like the indiscriminate killing of thousands of people.

"When you call somebody 'evil,' you also have to ask what kind of effect it has on you and the person you are talking about. Sometimes we call something 'evil' because we are afraid of it or do not understand it. The word can be used to dehumanize other people and justify all sorts of ugly or violent actions against them. When President Bush referred to other countries as an 'Axis of Evil,' it was like a threat, and it encouraged them to respond in ways that seemed threatening in return. Sometimes using the word 'evil' about someone can encourage exactly the kind of evil you are trying to avoid.

"I do not want to get in a fight with your mother, and I certainly do not want to call her evil, but her use of the word may not be very different from all the things that make her uncomfortable about President Bush."

One of the dangers of watching a documentary about the Revolutionary War with your five-year-old son is that the Redcoats might hang somebody, and questions will inevitably follow. This happened to my friend Danny. But he didn't take the easy way out—"Oh, he goes to sleep. And his soul leaves his body." He tried to answer, honestly, tactfully, with mixed success:

Gabriel: "Dad, why are they doing that to him?"
Danny: "To punish him."
Gabriel: "How does that punish him?"
Danny: "Well, when the horse rides away, the man will fall and hang from the rope."
Gabriel: (after a long pause) "What happens to the man when he hangs from the rope?"

Danny: (after an equally long pause) "He dies."

Gabriel: (more pausing) "How does he die?"

Danny: (beginning to sweat) "Well, I suppose he can't breathe because the rope is very tight around his neck."

Gabriel: "Then he dies?"

Danny: "Yeah."

Gabriel: "From not breathing?"

Danny: (desperate) "Yeah. Basically."

Let's bring in an expert.

"What happens to the man when he hangs from the rope?"

—GABRIEL SCHLACHET, age five, Brooklyn, New York

Frank Brown, coroner for Walla Walla County in Washington, one of two states that allow death-row inmates the option of being hanged (the other is New Hampshire):

"The first thing that happens is when the rope is placed around the neck, it is positioned to one side of the head, which is usually to the left side. What we are actually doing when someone is hung is rupturing the nerves and breaking the vertebral body—the cervical disks, the little bones in your neck. We are separating those. The knot is placed on that side of the neck because it gives a good directional pull. To the best of our knowledge, hanging is relatively pain-free because it is so quick that the body doesn't have a reaction time to the pain. It is not like they hang there and suffer. That isn't what happens. There is very little bleeding in the area. That is what we've seen with the autopsies that we've done.

"Now, if someone commits suicide in the shower or somewhere else at home by stepping off a chair, then you don't get that quick action. That is a different hanging episode. You get more of an inclusion, or stoppage of the arteries in the neck, that basically shuts off oxygen supply to the brain, and death occurs. There is a little more time needed for that to happen: instead of hundredths of a second, it's going to be seconds."

"Do you think he knows he's in there?"

—HALEY CALDWELL, age five, of Chardon, Ohio, as she patted the belly of her older cousin, who was pregnant

Dr. Kathleen Gustafson, associate director of the Fetal Biomagnetometry Laboratory, Hoglund Brain Imaging Center, University of Kansas Medical Center in Kansas City:

"Thankfully, no—if you knew you were in there, I think it would be kind of scary for nine months. The fetus is developing, of course, but the frontal lobe of our brain—the one that gives us emotion and self-recognition—develops very slowly. In fact, even up until adulthood, the frontal lobe isn't fully developed; that's partly why we sometimes see bad judgment in teenagers. I joke that parents are walking frontal lobes for their children.

"Now, infants do all sorts of wonderful exploring behavior in the womb. They run their hands along the inside of the womb, they feel their own feet, they feel their face, they start putting their hands in their mouth. Studies have also shown that a newborn infant will recognize its mother's voice versus a stranger's voice, and also recognize its native language versus a foreign language."

ME: *"But they don't think, Hey, I'm in my mother's stomach. Get me out of here!"*

"No. They don't even know who 'I' is."

"Why do people 'fall' in love? Do you always have to fall first?"

—MINA PAZ-LE DRAOULEC, age three, Hastings-on-Hudson, New York

Joyce Brothers, Ph.D., psychologist, advice columnist, television and radio host:

"We don't really fall in love; we jump in love—we are at the mercy of our chemical being. Chemicals are released in our brain when we are drawn to someone. The first, phenylethylamine, makes us feel very excited; everything is wonderful. It's almost like the flu: your face is flushed, your palms are sweaty, you are breathing heavy, you even feel a slight tingle in the hands and feet. We are attracted to opposites of ourselves—the organized person to the disorganized person, the bookworm to the social butterfly. We envy what we haven't got, and what we do is we jump into love to escape the possible loss of this person. We feel very jealous of somebody who has the characteristics we don't have, and we try to mold that person to us and become a couple.

"In the next stage, oxytocin is released. This is a hormone that plays an important role throughout our lives: it is sort of a cuddle hormone. Childbirth, a baby crying, makes it flow; nuzzling your baby makes it flow. Before that it acts as a kind of an infatuation chemical. Not only do we fall in love in this oxytocin time, but we can stay in love for a long time. The idea of romantic love is not something we have had forever, it is something that comes from the Middle Ages when knights started rescuing fair maidens in distress. It was men who cultivated this. Men fall in love pretty much by looks alone. They choose that way. Men fall in love after four dates; the average woman waits more than twenty dates. Women take much longer."

"What does 'sexy' mean?"

—AVA EISNER, age five, Merrick, New York

Eyvette Manigault, fitter and assistant manager, The Town Shop, Manhattan, who in thirty-six years on the job has fitted thousands of women for bras:

"It's the way a woman appears in front of someone, as far as the proper type of clothes she wears, and not having the clothes look sloppy on her. Very clean, stylish, not too tight, not too loose—say, as far as lingerie goes, sexy would mean a matching bra and panty set that is appropriate for a woman's shape. The right size bra: she can't be hanging over it, and it can't be so big on her. But it is not overdone or gaudy-looking—it is sexy-looking because it fits nice, it gives nice cleavage and uplift."

• • •

My dad has tried to help me with my quest for questions by asking colleagues and friends if their children had asked any good ones. "Here's one," he said one day. "Why are only the plastic plates and cups still wet when you take them out of the dishwasher?"

"That's great," I said. "Whose kid asked that?"

"No one's—I just want to know."

"Dad, it has to be a real question from a real kid."

"Oh, who'll know?"

"Dad!"

So he returned to the hunt. One friend told him that she had overheard the five-year-old son of a woman at the gym ask, "What is porn?" The mother's answer, alas, was not audible.

I asked my dad if he could get me the boy's full name. A few days later he called me back with it and suggested that with my journalistic skills, I should be able to find the family's phone number on my own.

I thanked him and began the process. I found the number easily enough by using an old reporting trick: I called 411. But as I started to dial, I imagined how the conversation could unfold:

"Hi. My name is Wendell Jamieson. I'm calling about [name of child]."

Child's mother: "Yes. What can I do for you?"

"Well, um, I'm writing a book in which I am finding expert answers to the questions of children."

"Yes."

"And I heard your son had a good one, and I'd like to include it, along with his full name."

"Uh-huh."

"The question was, 'What is porn?'"

"Is this some kind of joke?"

"No, it's not a joke."

"My son is five."

"I know, I know. That's what makes it funny. I just thought—"

"Funny? Does your publisher know you are harassing mothers with porn questions? Are you suggesting my husband and I watch porn? Do you know who my husband is?"

"Not really."

"Well, my husband is [name of husband]."

Thanks, Dad, but I think this is one case where I just won't use the kid's name.

"What is porn?"

—Unidentified boy, five or six, on the Upper East Side of Manhattan

Tricia Austin, vice president of marketing, *Penthouse* magazine:

"'Porn' is an informal use of the word 'pornography,' which applies to stories about and pictures of people who display their bodies and sometimes perform intimate acts publicly, to gain a strong reaction from an audience. It is as old as history itself, and has existed in many cultures: the Romans created pornographic images, and some Japanese woodblock prints from the nineteenth century could also be described as pornography. Pornography was even criminalized in Victorian England with the Obscene Publications Act of 1857, but today it is considered an accepted form of free speech in most societies. While porn may be considered an art form by some, just being naked is not porn. For example, there are classical paintings and statues of naked men and women displayed in museums around the world that show the human body simply for what it is . . . beautiful. Therefore, porn should be defined more by a viewer's reaction than solely the image of a nude body, or bodies. Either way, everyone agrees that pornography is something that is for adults only."

8.

The Strangest Species

To children, grown-ups are an unusual species, sharing the same house or apartment or trailer but governed by different rules and driven by curious motivations. We dress ourselves in odd garments and make jokes that aren't funny. We drink stinging amber-colored liquids and start laughing a lot, and we make a fuss over the joys of eating—not just fish, but sometimes even raw fish. We watch movies in which people talk a lot, but not much else seems to happen. We even criticize the president, who to a child looks like a genuinely nice man, a father, a lot of fun.

"Daddy, do you think I'll be president?" Dean once asked during breakfast.

"Do you want to be president?"

"Sure."

"You know, if you are president, you can't just do whatever

you want. You are in meetings all day, and you have to meet people who run countries that you've never heard of, and people write mean things about you in the newspaper."

"Do they always write mean things? Did newspapers write mean things about the other president, the one before Bush? What was his name?"

"Clinton? Yes, the newspapers wrote very mean things about him."

"Why?"

"Well, let's see. He kissed this girl named Monica. And he was married to somebody else. So he really shouldn't have. But then he lied about it. That was the worst thing. He got in really big trouble."

"I don't understand how you can get in trouble if you are the president. I mean, you are in charge—*you* are the president!"

"Yeah, but there's Congress."

"Who's he?"

Politics is just one strange facet of grown-up life. So many questions from children focus on the odd customs and doings of the adult world, from clothing to cocktails, from the things we buy to our ability to make seemingly arbitrary rules for them.

"Why do people buy things they don't need?"

"Why do grown-ups get to do what they want?"

"Why do men wear ties?"

Our entertainment choices get special attention: paintings with people just standing there; music with no discernible melodies; books with no pictures. Why do we find things so interesting that are so clearly boring?

At the top of the list has got to be movies with no action, no cartoons and, worst of all, no color. How can we watch such things? But I love movies, always have—ever since my dad took me to see Truffaut films in revival houses—and I want Dean to enjoy them with me. So on weekend nights he's allowed to stay up as long as he wants, to gain an insight into the secret nighttime world of grown-ups. The catch is that he has to watch a movie that Helene and I want to watch; we're not watching *Shark Boy and Lava Girl* after 9:00 p.m.

We look for movies that can be enjoyed on his level and on ours: he has seen *Sabrina*, and *To Kill a Mockingbird*, *Some Like It Hot* and *Bringing Up Baby.* He laughed out loud during *Monty Python and the Holy Grail.* He was riveted by *The Wind and the Lion*, in which Sean Connery plays an Arab chieftain with a Scottish accent and kidnaps Candice Bergen, who falls in love with him. I was riveted, too: my father took me and Lindsay to see this movie in the theater when it came out in 1975. He was having a fight with my mother and needed to get us out of the house.

Dean has seen samurai movies and French thrillers, which totally baffle him because he can't read fast enough for subtitles but that doesn't matter—he's happy to be awake when the rest of kid society is asleep, or should be. Of course, as the plots unfold in foreign languages, the questions come fast and furious.

Not too long ago, he stayed up with us to watch *Nightmare Alley*, starring Tyrone Power, a film noir from 1947 in which a carnival fortune-teller becomes a renowned spiritualist, only to end up in the gutter, in this case as the "geek"—the drunk side-show freak who bites off the heads of chickens for an amazed crowd. Dean was silent throughout, not a single question, and I figured he'd passed out: dialogue-heavy black-and-white melodramas, I've found, can act as highly effective sleep agents for children. The apartment was dark except for the gray glow of the screen, and then completely black when I shut off the television.

But then I switched on the lights. Dean was wide awake.

He looked at me and asked one question:

"What was that movie about?"

That got me thinking. I knew what had happened in the movie, knew the plot, but Dean seemed to be asking a deeper question. What, truly, was it about? What was the director trying to tell us?

So I went in search of a movie director, someone who doesn't only make movies, but has an intuitive love of the art's history, whose movies themselves reflect that love. *Paper Moon* got a very good reception during one of our late weekend nights—it's an adult movie, black-and-white, but the heroine is a ten-year-old girl grifter, played by Tatum O'Neal. Dean seemed to feel some kinship with her, although he was scandalized when she smoked a cigarette.

I got in touch with *Paper Moon* director Peter Bogdanovich for an explanation of *Nightmare Alley.* I was hoping for not just a plot synopsis, but an answer that would put the film in a little more context, for both me and my son, as well as an insightful critical analysis.

It's always fun to get a famous person on the telephone: they sound thrillingly like they do on screen. Bogdanovich has a deep, resonant voice. He said he was fully prepared for the question. When he was young, he explained, he went to the movies obsessively and took notes. He filled out a card with a brief description of every movie he saw, and rated each one. All he had to do was pull out his *Nightmare Alley* card, which was apparently dated.

"I saw it on a double bill with *Thieves' Highway* in 1955," he said.

My dad and I had seen that film at a revival house a few months earlier. It stars Richard Conte as a truck driver hauling apples to San Francisco, bent on revenge against the warehouse boss who crippled his father. It contains a startlingly beautiful shot of hundreds of apples rolling down a hillside in the dappled morning sunshine, and the children of the apple growers scrambling to retrieve them.

"That's a great movie," I said of *Thieves' Highway.*

"No—that's a good movie, not a great movie," Bogdanovich said, with some authority. "I wouldn't say it's a great movie. But it had some great things in it."

"Like those apples rolling down the hill," I said.

"Yes, those apples."

Here we got into a long discussion of that film's plot, and our confusion about Conte's love interest, a woman who lived alone in a dreary room near the fruit and vegetable wholesalers. "That was very strange. She must have been a prostitute, don't you think?" he asked me. I wasn't sure.

Bogdanovich then read his review of *Nightmare Alley.* It was highly critical. He laughed at his younger self as he read. "Boy, I really didn't like it," he said when he was done.

I enjoyed our chat. But what has stuck with me even more than his answer to Dean's question was his method of teaching himself to make movies: going to them, obsessively, and writing down not only what he saw, but how he felt about it. He was only a kid, but he took himself as seriously as if he were the reviewer for *The New York Times.* He filled up those index cards. But at the same time, he was still learning—he excitedly picked my brain about an obscure plot point (the prostitute) in an obscure movie.

I wondered: What will Dean love that much?

At their darkest cores, *Thieves' Highway* and *Nightmare Alley* are both about one thing: money—the lengths people will go to, and what they will give up, to acquire it. Tyrone Power surrenders his soul and becomes a con man; Richard Conte's father, desperate for income, loses his legs.

To a child, the handling, discussion and procurement of money is one of the most riveting aspects of the adult world—it can be exchanged for all sorts of wonderful things, from toy trucks to Power Rangers to sneakers with Velcro; too bad Dad has to spend all week at the office, sometimes late, to get it. Coins and dollars are covered with symbols and codes, pictures of people and places, all needing explanation.

Not too long ago, I gave Dean a front-row seat as a pair of male human adults engaged in a strange mental contest over this fascinating commodity. The experience taught me that there was only one drawback to Dean being able to speak clearly, and that was the fact that he was able to speak clearly. Some things you just don't want to do with a question-happy—not to mention, honest—little boy, and at the very top of the list is trading in your old car for a new one.

It was finally time to replace our 1991 light blue Honda Accord, which I had bought from my mother when it had 62,000 miles on the odometer, just before Dean was born. In the subsequent months and years we had driven him home from the hospital in it, driven him around the midnight streets to calm his colic in it, taken it out to the cottage on Long Island in the summers, and generally banged it up on the streets of New York City. Now there were 114,000 miles on the odometer.

The Honda had become something of a sore spot between Dean and myself. It was covered with a patina of dents and scratches, a faded paper parking violation was permanently pasted to the left rear window, the carpet was embedded with sand, and someone little had slipped a fistful of quarters into a square hole on the top of the steering column; the quarters couldn't be found—two mechanics tried—but they could always be heard, noisily cascading like a stream of winnings from a slot machine every time we turned a corner or went over a bump.

"Daddy, why is our car so old?" Dean would ask me from his booster seat. All kinds of crap was around him: groceries, a stroller, some old clothes I was supposed to take to the Salvation Army, and all the tools one needs to raise and transport a child these days. His eyes filled the rearview mirror.

"It's not old," I said.

"Well, it's a little old."

"Okay. It's a little old. But it runs great! Hondas, you know, you can put two hundred thousand miles on them. They are great cars."

"But it's a little old."

I was defending my automotive pride to a five-year-old. And I was losing.

"A little."

The traffic budged. I turned the corner. The steering column went *Ka-ching! Ka-ching! Ka-ching!*

When Helene and I were dating, we bought (for $200) a really old car, a 1974 Triumph TR6, that we drove down to the Jersey Shore for one summer before it developed a worrisome tilt after hitting a pothole and our mechanic, Howie, told us that the H-frame was rusted through and had broken in two places. It had been a short but intense love affair, our time with the TR6, the air over the windshield golden with sun and heavy with the smell of salt water as we got nearer to the ocean after leaving work early on Friday afternoons.

Now a parent, more than ten years later, I was forced to admit that not only were my British sports-car days over, but so, too, were my slot-machine Honda days. I was entering my station wagon era—I needed a place to put all the child-care tools and devices that were piled on top of Dean.

I was experiencing the same emotions that my father, who had once owned a Jaguar XK120, had felt when he bought that Volkswagen station wagon, the one with the engine in the back. At least mine would have the engine in the front, I figured, and would benefit from all the important technical innovations of the last thirty-five years, like air-conditioning.

Online research convinced me that a used Volvo V40 was the way to go. I found the year and color and (nearly) the price I wanted at a dealership nearby, one that handled both Hondas and Volvos; I figured I could drive in with one and out with the other.

I planned my negotiating tactics carefully. I would offer to write a check right there on the spot from my home-equity account, no need to finance, so they'd probably give me a break on the price. I knew all about the car, its specs, etc., so I wouldn't be taking up more than a few minutes of anyone's time. And of course I had the Honda. I determined online that its trade-in value was $1,000. That should work fine.

On the big day, to put the old car in her best possible light, Dean and I got her cleaned in a hand carwash. She nearly sparkled in the sun as she got toweled off in the parking lot.

The Volvo salesman was named Ronald Charles. He had a picture of his police-officer daughter on his desk. He seemed like a good guy and I decided that he was someone I could do business with. Yes, he said, they still had the blue V40 I wanted on the lot, yes, they would be happy to take the Honda as a trade-in and, sure, it would be great if I could just write the check right there. Dean and I went out and looked at it, played with the sun and moon roofs and heated seats, and he gave his nod of approval. He was especially taken with the spring-loaded automatic cup holder.

Back in the showroom, Ron and I got down to business. I gave him the VIN number for the Honda—1HGCB7540MA180450—and he punched it into a computer. "Is this car clean?" he asked me.

"Sure it's clean. My mother sold it to me. You think my mother would sell me a hot car?"

"No no." He laughed, shaking his head. I was charming him. I could sense the price coming down even as we spoke. Dean watched us.

Ron said: "Has this car ever been in an accident?"

"No."

Dean's eyes went wide. "Daddy," he said in a stage whisper. I tried to ignore him.

"Daddy—remember that time. The bumper?"

Ron looked up from his computer. "The bumper?"

"Daddy—you remember."

A year earlier, while driving Dean, his sister and my mother-in-law to a barbecue in New Jersey in stop-and-go traffic, I had tapped—just tapped—the bumper of the car ahead of me when I turned around for a half-second to shut up everyone in the backseat. The driver of the impact vehicle and I got out, looked at our bumpers and got back into our cars to continue our journeys. Nothing was exchanged beyond dirty looks. It was no big deal. I told Ron this story.

"No no," Dean said. "Not that time—you know, *the bumper.* The time it got ripped off? The truck?"

Oh, haha, right. I'd once parked the car on a corner, and a truck had turned a little too tightly and torn off the front bumper and the front lights and part of the radiator and flattened both front tires.

"Is there anything else?" Ron said.

"Nope."

He got up, we did, too, and we all went out back to have a look at the sparkling Honda. "Try not to say anything else," I told Dean.

Ron's general manager came out to inspect it, got in the front seat, turned the steering wheel. *Ka-ching!*

"What the hell is that?"

"Um, change," I said.

Dean looked away for a second and I pointed accusingly at the back of his head, making sure Ron and his general manager knew who was the culprit responsible for all the loose change in the steering column.

We all went back inside. Dean and I sat at Ron's desk, under the gaze of his police-officer daughter, while Ron and the general manager huddled on the other side of the showroom. They were probably trying to figure out just how low they could go. I got out my checkbook. I told Dean to pay attention—he might learn something. "Now we're gonna haggle," I said.

"Haggle?"

"Yeah. It means compromise. I'm feeling good about this."

Ron came back.

"Listen, that car of yours, that Honda."

"Yeah?"

"It's a donation case."

"A donation case?"

"You know, something you can give to charity. We couldn't sell it. But my general manager says, you know, we don't want to insult you, so maybe we can give you three hundred for it."

"Oh. Hmmm. Okay. So you know, I can write that check right now, no financing, if maybe you guys can go a little lower."

"Oh no," Ron said. He smiled firmly. "No. The price is fourteen thousand nine hundred ninety-five, minus the three hundred."

We don't want to insult you.

I tried to keep my poker face, tried to think of a new tactic, but then an attack came from an unexpected quarter.

Dean said: "Daddy, are you trying to pay less money for this car?"

Ron followed right on cue: "Daddy, are you trying to pay less money for this car?"

I was outnumbered. I sighed as I felt my internal engine run down. So I opened my checkbook.

"Who do I make it out to?"

"If we had a trillion dollars, would we be the same people?"

—ALISON SHARON, age ten, Rancho Santa Margarita, California

Brad Duke, Boise, Idaho, who won $220.3 million in the May 2005 Powerball Multi-State Lottery:

"Yes, you would be the same people. But it would take a little bit of work to stay the same people, because the perceptions of the people around you will change. You have to be true to yourself, with your own mind, your own heart, to ignore whatever other people think based on you having a trillion dollars. People will react to you in different ways, from jealousy to admiration to awe to frustration, or even being angry because you have money that they don't have.

"Let me give you an example. I played the lottery a lot: it was a hobby of mine, a numbers game. I just wanted to see how close I could come to matching the numbers. After I won, I was asked if I had ever thought I was going to win. I said, 'Oh, yeah. It's a hobby. I wouldn't be surprised if I won again.' To some people, that was offensive. Someone took my picture out of the paper and put it under a piece of glass at the grocery store and wrote on it with a Sharpie: 'GREED PERSONIFIED.' Well, they don't know that I still live in the same house, that I drive a used car.

"I get lots of requests for weird things, like money to build a time machine. I got one handwritten note that I keep in my wallet: 'I am a hardworking Minnesota girl but I messed up my checking account and I need some money. Ten thousand dollars. Please, please, please, please.' I keep it to remind me about people's perceptions of me."

ME: *"Did you have to fight the urge to change? Did you find yourself saying, 'Well, I really don't need a Rolls-Royce, but now that I can afford it, maybe I'll buy one'?"*

"One thing that I learned very quickly is that the lure of having that nice house, that nice car, well, the attraction of that is more when you can't have it than when you can. It's cool to have the ability to do it, but it is cooler not to do it. I had no problem fighting those urges."

"Why do people buy things they don't need?"

—ELLA HESTER, age seven, Brooklyn, New York

Sandra Heiman, Hudson Valley, New York, who suffers from compulsive shopping disorder:

"People who over-shop or spend compulsively think that they need the items they buy at the time they purchase them. These people are often trying to distract themselves from feelings that are painful to them, such as loneliness, low self-esteem, anger, hurt, loss . . . among others. It starts off as a fun thing to do, one that brings pleasure. But eventually shopping starts to control the person rather than the other way around. For these people, over-shopping or buying things they don't need can become self-destructive, like any addiction, and cause problems in the person's family and relationships."

ME: *"What's the craziest thing you ever bought? Something that you looked at the next day and were like, 'What's this? I don't need this.'"*

"I never really felt that I didn't need it. I am very practical about what I buy. I buy things that are pretty or beautiful or high quality. I may run across a pair of shoes after I've had a dress or an outfit for years and think, 'Wow, this would be great.' I used shopping to distract me from pain, or loneliness or emptiness. Even if I didn't buy the item and bring it home the next day, I would put it on layaway and I'd think about it and it made me feel better."

"So what kind of things were you buying?"

"Jewelry, shoes, clothing mostly, maybe some makeup. It started out when money was more fluid, and then when money got cut back, I still had the need without the means. Then I started to do things that were dishonest to get them. I'd find a way to get the money. I never stole. Somebody else would look at me and say, 'Why does she need another pair of shoes? Why does she need another dress?' But for me, I just needed it."

"Why does a dollar sign have an S in it?"

—STELLA HACKETT, age seven, Brooklyn, New York

Richard Doty, curator, National Numismatics Collection, National Museum of American History, Washington:

"It is most likely from Spanish notation—it's shorthand, basically, for pesos. Our dollars started out as pesos, which means 'pieces of eight.' When we were colonies we were trading bootleg with the Spanish Empire and we were getting pieces of eight, and that became the genesis for the American dollar. Paper money in Maryland actually showed a piece of eight on the one-dollar bill. One way of writing pesos was having a 'p' with a couple of downstrokes, and then the loop around, and over time, I think, personally, it evolved into the 'S' with the lines through it we see today."

"Why does the pyramid on the dollar bill have an eye in it?"

—DEAN

Doug Mudd, curator of exhibitions for the American Numismatic Association Money Museum, Colorado Springs, Colorado:

"The pyramid-and-eye design for the back of the dollar bill is based on the Great Seal of the United States, originally designed during the American Revolution. It has its origins in Masonic imagery. The eye is the all-seeing eye of Providence, representing a Masonic view of the universal power, whether you call it God or providence. It was specifically chosen to symbolize the intervention of providence in favor of the American cause during the revolution. The Freemasons believed that there is a being that sees everything, that encompasses everything in its awareness, and many of the Founding Fathers were Masons. The current one-dollar design was introduced in 1935 on Silver Certificates at a time when the events and symbols of the American Revolution were on people's minds—just after the 150th anniversary events and at a time of hardship (the Great Depression)."

"What was that movie about?"

—DEAN, after seeing the 1947 film noir *Nightmare Alley* with me

Peter Bogdanovich, director of numerous movies, including *Paper Moon* and *The Last Picture Show*:

"I haven't seen the picture since 1955, which is a few years ago. From 1952 through '70, I kept a card on every movie I saw. I typed it up. I usually did it right after I saw it. I'd grade it and then I'd write something about it. If I saw it again, and I had a new opinion, I'd write the new opinion. I didn't like [*Nightmare Alley*]. Would you like to hear it? I gave it a fair-minus rating. 'Weird, not very believable carnival story mixed with vaguely surrealistic psychological mystery ending with the hero becoming a "geek" who must eat live chickens in the sideshow. Murky, badly acted, silly and pointless, it nevertheless evokes a rather fascinating atmosphere of nightmarish reality.' "

"Why in exciting movies is the most exciting part always at the end?"

—DEAN, after watching *The Wind and the Lion*, the 1975 adventure film starring Sean Connery and Candice Bergen

John Milius, writer and director, *The Wind and the Lion*:

"It's like a piece of music—you have to reach a crescendo. Art has always been that way: music is that way, plays are that way. Fireworks always have the best stuff at the end, don't they? Part of it is to keep you sitting there until the end of the movie; you think there will be more and more of that intensity, the movie has to top itself. It may even be primal. It's like sex, because sex is that way, building, and we are so driven by our primal urges. At the end of *The Wind and the Lion*, I threw in everything—you had Germans with spiked helmets, the horses charging. But the real ending is after that, when Connery's character escapes and he's riding his horse and he leans down and takes the rifle from the kid. That is sort of the high point; you can't go any further.

"I find today whenever I see a film the action goes on forever, and it is all overdone. I remember on my first film, *Dillinger*, I had these guys blazing away with machine guns, and buildings were falling down, and there were bullet hits and bodies flying and splattering blood, and I realized that a little of that goes a long way. You can't have an awful lot because you become sated very quickly; it loses its impact."

ME: *"I just have to ask: Sean Connery's Scottish accent. It seemed so incongruous, coming from an Arab, when he first speaks. After that you don't notice. Did you discuss his accent during casting? While you were planning the film?"*

"We spent about six weeks having him trained to speak in an Arab manner, with an Arab accent. But after that, when he spoke to me in an Arab accent, all I heard was a Scottish burr. Nothing had changed. So I just figured that whoever taught his character to speak English was a Scot. I remember one of the reviews—my movies never got good reviews—in which John Simon just couldn't get past Sean Connery's accent. I realized that there was no point worrying about what these guys said. I became immunized to reviews."

"What movie played the longest in theaters?"

—ELLA HESTER, age eight, Brooklyn, New York

Sid Ganis, president, Academy of Motion Picture Arts and Sciences, Beverly Hills, California:

"I'd say it's *Gone With the Wind.* Over the years, since it opened in the late 1930s, it's been revived many, many times, including ten years ago when they restored the negative. They didn't keep these kinds of statistics when it first came out and the industry was much different: a theatrical run was the only run—there wasn't television, and even when there was television, at first, there were still no movies on television. There was no VHS and certainly no DVD and cable and that stuff. The main form of distribution for movies was in a movie theater. So movies were in the theater much longer."

Me: *"Do you think it has anything to do with the movie itself?"*

"Yes, yes. There is something about *Gone With the Wind* that is absolutely captivating: the look of the movie, the sound of the movie and, when you get into it, the story of the movie. Two or three months ago I happened to come across it on television somewhere in the middle, and I didn't leave for another hour and a half. It's iconic, but iconic for all the right reasons: it is splendid storytelling, it is splendid moving-picture fare."

"Why do grown-ups get to do what they want?"

—MARLEY-ROSE LIBBURD, age five, Brooklyn, New York

Nathan L. Hecht, senior justice, Supreme Court of Texas:

"It only seems that way to young people because adults make all the rules. Actually, the law applies more strictly to adults than minors. All states and most countries set an age, usually between eighteen and twenty-one, below which a person gets special treatment. Minors can't be held to their contracts and are sometimes excused for injuring others. Minors who commit crimes are usually treated as delinquents and punished less severely than adults. The reason is that minors do not have the breadth of life's experiences to appreciate the consequences of their choices. Adults do not have the same excuse. They can't do whatever they want but must follow the law or pay the penalty. Part of being grown-up is making wise choices, so that what you want, what's good for you and what the law allows are all the same things."

"Can thirteen-year-olds get their own apartments?"

—LILY KOPPEL, age thirteen, Chicago

Judy Roettig, executive vice president of the Chicagoland Apartment Association, a trade association representing landlords:

"A thirteen-year-old can't rent her own apartment because contract law dictates that the signatory on a lease must be eighteen years or older. Now here's an interesting sidebar: should the landlord want to evict you, and you are thirteen years old, you *are* old enough to receive service of a notice of eviction. You have to be twelve or older to accept the notice. So thirteen-year-olds can't pay the rent, but are old enough to accept notice if their parents don't."

"Why do men wear ties?"

—TONY MUIA, age three, Brooklyn, New York

Massimo Ferragamo, chairman of the United States division of Salvatore Ferragamo, which sold 27,000 ties worldwide in 2005:

"Men wear ties because it's a convention imposed on them from a very early age. In fact, the convention of wearing something around one's neck seems to have existed for hundreds of years. The tie is thought to be an evolution of the neck scarf, cravat, lace collar and bandanna, all of which have been worn by men at certain points in history. But what I find interesting about a tie is that it's synonymous with the uniform, yet is one of the few ways a man can express his individuality when formally attired."

"Why does the chef wear that big white hat?"

—DEAN

Georges Perrier, chef and owner, Le Bec-Fin restaurant, Philadelphia (speaking with a very thick French accent that makes "hat" sound like "at"):

"First of all, I think, in the old times we all wore hats for health reasons. And the *chef de cuisine,* his hat was higher and bigger, and the other ones were smaller. We call it a 'toque.' It shows he's the boss, he's in charge. And his hat would have—how you say?—pleats. Those pleats mean how many years he's been in the restaurant, how old a chef he is. This is the old tradition but now it is a different story. In my restaurant I don't wear a hat. I should, out of respect for my profession, but I don't. When I go to meet the master chefs in France, when we all get together, then we wear our hats. I think it's beautiful to see the chefs with their hats. But with me, the ceiling in my kitchen is low, so I can't wear a tall hat. Everyone who works there, everyone in the kitchen, they wear a casket."

ME: *"A casket?"*

"Yes, you know, a casket? Do you understand? Wait a minute. [He speaks in French to someone near him in the kitchen before coming back to the telephone.] I mean a cap. Everyone in the kitchen has to wear a cap. This is for sanitary reasons."

"Why do dancers change their clothes for the samba?"

—CECE STURMAN, age three, Los Angeles, California, while watching *Strictly Ballroom*

Carlinhos de Jesus, renowned samba dancer who choreographs the opening act of Mangueira, one of the most traditional samba schools to participate in Rio de Janeiro's annual Carnival parade:

"It depends on the style of samba they're dancing. Brazilian *sambistas*, as the samba dancers are known there, practice two styles: the *samba no pé*, which literally means "foot samba," and the *samba de gafieira*, or ballroom samba, which couples dance together in nightclubs, just like they would dance the rumba or the fox-trot. This is not the same samba that we see in international ballroom-dance competitions, though. The international ballroom samba doesn't exist in Brazil and it really doesn't look or sound at all like the Brazilian samba. It is, instead, a mix of Latin rhythms that was popularized abroad by Carmen Miranda, the Portuguese-Brazilian performer who sang and danced it on Broadway and in many Hollywood movies in the 1940s.

"There's no specific clothing for the *samba no pé*, but the women like to wear tight shirts and miniskirts so as to accentuate the movement of their legs and hips. Because this style is danced during the annual Carnival parade in Rio de Janeiro, the clothing will depend on the theme selected by each samba school that participates in the parade. The dancers wear costumes that are representative of the theme, like fish-shaped hats, for example, if the school is honoring something related to the ocean. For the *samba de gafieira*, the men wear striped T-shirts, panama hats and white linen suits that are evocative of Rio de Janeiro's bohemians, while the women wear elegant dresses and high-heel shoes. These clothes are more elegant because the *gafieira*, or ballroom, is a social place—a place where a man would take a woman he likes to dance at night, to have a good time.

"Dancers of the international ballroom samba are usually inspired by Carmen Miranda and her extravagant clothing: flowing skirt, tight bustier, platform shoes. These clothes are often pretty colorful, like the plastic fruits and birds that Carmen Miranda used to have on the turbans she wore in the movies and which are so characteristic of Brazil."

"Why do you have girl hair?"

—TYLER KENT, age five, Pensauken, New Jersey, while eating in a diner with his uncle, who had a ponytail

Carol Pershing, studio hairstylist, head of the hair department for HBO's *Deadwood*, for which she won an Emmy:

"Men used to have long hair because they didn't always have barbers and it wasn't easy to get their hair cut. In England, they used to have the curls and they were also very coiffed and stuff. At the time of *Deadwood*, in the old American

West, they would just let it grow and grow and grow. There was a barber, and a lot of times they would go in for special occasions and get their beards trimmed or cut or their hair cut, but it wasn't done weekly; they barely took a bath once a week. Grooming themselves was not a big thing. When hair got shorter, in the twenties, it was because of lice; they started cutting the hair really down because people would get lice. When it got longer in the sixties, it just was part of that hippie thing, of kind of letting yourself go and doing your own thing and not conforming. Really, shorter hair represents being a little more uptight. But some men just like having long hair, the feel of it. You can also put it in a ponytail, where it is kept under control but the person's other side—their fun side—is there, too; they are more individual, into their own thing."

"Why can't I pick my nose in front of other people?"

—ELLIOT APPLEBAUM, age seven, La Jolla, California

Peter Post, director of the Emily Post Institute, and great-grandson of Emily Post, who first published her seminal guide to etiquette in 1922:

"Because it's gross. Why is it gross? Well, what's gross is that you are taking something gooey and disgusting out of your nose, and then you have to do something with it. If you eat it, you are going to make other people's stomachs turn upside down. If you stick it under a table, it's pretty grotesque—people are going to see it, touch it, feel it in the future. Finally, even if you use a tissue and get it off your finger, your finger is going to touch other people. The problem is, when we pick our nose, we think we've done it very surreptitiously—nobody saw it, so it's okay. But usually somebody sees it, and from other people's perspective it's really vile.

"The easiest thing to do is just to excuse yourself and do it in the privacy of a bathroom or anyplace where you won't force other people to watch. We are basically social animals. We like to get along with other people. And part of getting along with other people—and this is the core essence of what etiquette is all about—is treating people with consideration and respect and honesty. And the problem with picking your nose in front of other people is that it can make them uncomfortable. Etiquette is really about building relationships, and if we want to have a great relationship with people, we should temper some of that picking of the nose. That's why we have table manners: not to gross out people while we eat. Same concept. We don't chew with our mouths open because nobody wants to see that mash of goo chewing around in our mouths."

"Who invented homework?"

—STEPHEN DINISO, age ten, Floral Park, New York

Steven Schlossman, Ph.D., Department of History, Carnegie Mellon University:

"We know very little about the origins of homework, except to say that for hundreds of years it was a staple of upper-grammar and secondary schooling, and that it was integral to the predominant style of teaching that stressed drill, memorization and recitation; children had to prepare furiously the night before to 'say their lessons' in school.

"A more interesting question for modern kids might be: Who invented homework for very young children? If there is anything radically new on the educational scene today, it is the idea that homework is as good for children in the early grades as for students in high school. Indeed, nowadays homework assignments in kindergarten are increasingly common.

"This practice runs wholly against the conventional wisdom of most twentieth-century educational, psychological and medical experts, who viewed homework as bad for young children's health—mentally, emotionally, even physically—anytime before the third grade. It also runs up against the best scientific evidence available today about the impact of homework on school achievement: very positive effects in high school, marginally beneficial in middle school, but of least—if any—benefit in the early grades. So far, there's no solid evidence that getting habituated to homework early does children good."

My mother eventually came to run a jewelry school. She has a gallery show once a year on the East Side of Manhattan. The sound of her hammering away in her studio in our house in Park Slope is one of the most evocative audio memories of my childhood. So when this question came along, I knew exactly where to go for the answer. Mom?

"What do they do with the shavings?"

—NANCY DILLON, age seven, San Carlos, California, after being given a gold ring that had been engraved

Bessie Jamieson, owner of the Jewelry Arts Institute, New York City:

"You save every little bit of shavings—we call them filings—and recycle them. You sell them back to a refiner. I take them to a person who refines gold on Forty-seventh Street, a guy named Lee, at Marco Polo. I take all my filings and pieces of scrap, have them melted down, assayed—that's tested—and refined. He charges me to do that, but he gives me back the gold that's in them. So if I take in ten ounces of filings, I might get six ounces of pure gold back. Also, I take in the sweep from the floor and from the desks, too, and they refine that. They melt it all down and throw away what isn't gold, and whatever's left is mine. Years ago—I don't know if they still do it—shops that made jewelry that had wooden floors, they took up the floors and burned them to get the gold out of the wood."

9.

Deanosaurus

It started with a dog-eared picture book and a few plastic dinosaur figures Dean found in the back of the classroom. Who knows what he saw when he first gazed at those prehistoric beasts, and began to wrestle with the idea that they had once lived here, and now were gone, and that no human had ever seen them, and yet here were their pictures. Whatever it was, it sparked something deep within him.

For Christmas, my sister sent Dean a whole selection of dinosaur figures. It included all the classics: *Tyrannosaurus rex*, *Stegosaurus*, *Triceratops*, *Ankylosaurus*, *Brontosaurus* and a few more. Other dinosaur books and other figures followed, given by friends and family. There were pop-up books, and books with cutaway pages on clear plastic, and encyclopedias that listed every imaginable kind of beast, from every era, and were almost too heavy for a five-year-old to lift.

Then came the DVDs, with realistic-looking carnivores chasing panicked herbivores over rocky terrain or through thickly wooded glades. *Jurassic Park* went into heavy rotation on the DVD player, the scary parts fast-forwarded or blocked, tiny hands over big brown eyes.

The living room, no longer a traffic jam, became a prehistoric battleground. Dean set up the death matches around our feet. He was especially interested in various dinosaurs' defenses, and their offensive characteristics—teeth, horns, claws, those visible tools that plunged into the necks of dinner, or drove deep into the soft bellies of attackers. He wanted to know how they worked, what all those fantastic instruments were designed to do. He focused on their visible tools, their systems, just as my friend Gia in New Brunswick had said little boys are apt to do.

His interest had phases and subsets: first it was long necks, then *Velociraptors*, then *Ankylosaurus* and then *Pachycephalosaurus.* Never duckbills, for which he seemed to have a certain scorn, saying they looked silly and couldn't defend themselves. Each subset had its own progression: he would learn about this dinosaur, what made it different, then he'd start drawing it, surprisingly well, in much the same way as Peter Bogdanovich described and organized all the movies he saw on index cards, taking possession of them at an early age. Dean developed impressive physical imitations of the stances he saw in books, and even created sounds to go with the images. It wasn't clear where he came up with this; Helene and I wondered if dinosaur impersonations could lead to a career.

One day when I was off work, I stopped by the schoolyard during recess, looking for my now kindergarten-age son amid the screaming hordes on the other side of the fence. I scanned the yard, starting at the edges. As I did, I became conscious of a secret fear, similar to those no doubt harbored by other parents: I began to worry that all the kids would be playing tag but Dean would be off in some distant corner, wailing like a *Protoceratops.*

It had rained in the morning; boys and girls nonchalantly jumped wide puddles, their mirror images flicking across them. They seemed like a good group of kids, all clean and nicely dressed. There were no crap games unfolding in the schoolyard's distant corners with dice-throwing six-year-olds cursing a blue streak, stubby unlit cigars sticking out of their mouths. This was encouraging. So I moved my eyes to the center, and there Dean was, running around with his cronies, laughing and screaming, no faux-prehistoric yelps or shrieks coming from his mouth. He broke free to come see me for a few moments, fingers gripping the chain-link fence, and then rejoined the mob.

Those two boys in the local library who knew the planets? By now I had started to see in Dean what Helene had seen in them: a bottomless interest, a desire for knowledge for knowledge's sake. Not only was Dean's speech improving every day—except for a brief period near the end of kindergarten when he developed what can only be described as a thick French accent—but he was drinking in information, keeping it and processing it.

We read; he retained. He learned Triassic, Jurassic and Cretaceous, and herbivore, carnivore and omnivore. I can only imagine that a young mother who bumped into Helene and him as they pored over dinosaur books in the library would have been alarmed at her own child's progress, and run home demanding swift action. Dean's birthday parties had a dinosaur theme: Helene painted a giant mural of dinosaurs and hung it across the bookcase—"HAPPY BIRTHDAY DINO"—and I was off to The Ice House, two years running, in search of dry ice for the volcano cake.

And the questions multiplied.

"Why do little kids love T-rex?" Dean asked me when he was five, thinking back to the days when he had been four.

"I guess because he's the biggest," I said.

"But he's not," Dean answered. "*Spinosaurus* is bigger, and *Giganotosaurus*, too."

"Maybe because he's the scariest?"

"But he's not. *Dilophosorus*, the one with the neck that comes out, the one from *Jurassic Park* that spits poison? He's scarier."

"Maybe it's because he had those weird little arms with those nasty little fingers on them."

"Yeah, that's it."

Here he did his imitation—crouch-leaning forward, legs bent, fingers curled into hideous talons.

I knew the answer because I'd had my own dinosaur phase. This was post-cranes, pre-ships, an interest that had faded, even been forgotten, until Dean rekindled it. I, too, had wrestled with the mind-blowing concept of our planet—including the land on which our city sat—being inhabited by a universe of animals that had long since died out, and had never been seen.

Of course, a lot had changed with dinosaurs in the intervening thirty years. When I was little, there were about nine of them; now there were hundreds. Once slow, small-brained and hand-drawn, dinosaurs were now fantastically streamlined and agile, computer-generated, armed with giant single claws and all manner of spikes and spines, festooned with sails and crests and sprouting brightly colored plumage. Their systems had gone mad. They hunted in packs, moved like lightning, fought like demons. There were countless variations and subsets, all going by longer and longer and more unpronounceable names, many of them Chinese.

I also discovered that the packaging in which dinosaur toys came had also undergone a transformation. Once tossed inside flimsy cardboard boxes with crinkly plastic windows for viewing, they were now lashed in place by translucent wires of titanium-like strength tied in unfathomable knots, anchored to black plastic bases with dozens of microscopic Phillips-head screws. It could take hours to free them.

In the middle of Dean's early dinosaur phase, my mother shocked Lindsay and me by selling the house in Park Slope. I'd liked the idea of having that house around, even if I didn't live in it, even if a few bad memories hung around all that beautiful mahogany woodwork. The idea of it being sold to another family was somehow very painful. Still, I steadied my nerves and went over to help clear out the week before the closing, and that's when I came across *The How and Why Wonder Book of Dinosaurs.*

Torn at the corners from overuse, the cover showed a scowling *Brontosaurus* hip-deep in water on a soupy prehistoric day, with a T-rex dragging its tail along a distant shore, a *Pterodactyl* gliding by a giant palm tree and a volcano erupting above another wading *Brontosaurus* in the far distance. This had been my favorite book when I was Dean's age.

I stared at the cover. Sitting cross-legged on the wooden floor, books and photographs and college papers piled around me, I began to flip through the pages as my mother and sister yelled to each other through the glass-paneled doors—the sound traveling through the still-empty rectangle where the kicked pane once had been—deciding what should be tossed and what should be saved. The black-and-white drawings captured roughly a dozen smooth-skinned, lumbering dinosaurs in various stages of eating, foraging, fighting or being consumed, and prompted a surprisingly strong feeling of involuntary memory in me: they seemed so familiar, these pictures, even though it had been three decades since I'd seen them.

The contours of a *Triceratops* impaling a rigidly upright T-rex seemed to fit into a missing spot in my psyche, like the last piece of a puzzle.

The drawing of a long-necked *Diplodocus*—I pronounced it dip-lo-DOCK-us—invoked something even more unusual, an involuntary audio memory. As soon as I turned the page to it, the song "Summer Breeze" played in my head: *Summer breeze, makes me feel fine . . .*

This strange association precisely dated my dinosaur phase to July or August 1972, when the song, by a band called Seals & Crofts, was a hit, propelled up the charts by its catchy if cheesy guitar part and stoned lyrics.

It's funny how a dinosaur and a riff will do that. One minute you're a thirty-eight-year-old man in his old room looking through a book, wondering what to throw away, the debris of your childhood all around you, and the next you're a little boy with a big head of hair, sun-bleached and sand-covered, sitting in the backseat of your family's old Volkswagen station wagon, and the radio is playing. Your parents are up front, still together, impossibly young, your sister is next to you, impossibly younger, a book is in your lap and summer is outside the window.

I took *The How and Why Wonder Book of Dinosaurs* back to show Dean what dinosaurs looked like when I was little. He saw the cover and got excited, but as he flipped through the pages, I detected a loss of enthusiasm; he seemed to be deflating. He kept coming up to me, the book opened in his hands, his finger pointing.

"T-rex didn't drag his tail like that."

"*Brachiosaurus* couldn't breathe underwater."

"*Allosaurus* didn't live at the same time as *Triceratops.* One was Jurassic, one was Cretaceous."

I flipped the page to the *Diplodocus.*

"How about *Diplodocus,* is this right?" I asked him.

He looked at me and said: "It's dih-PLOD-uh-kuss."

Our default weekend destination had become the American Museum of Natural History on the Upper West Side of Manhattan. A castle of rough granite, towers and soaring columns on Central Park, it contains some of the greatest dinosaur fossil specimens ever unearthed. My mother took my sister and me here again and again when we were little, the dinosaur halls dark and almost dingy, unchanged for fifty years. But they underwent a redesign in the early 1990s to become as radically altered from my childhood as toy dinosaurs and toy-dinosaur packaging—sunlight pours in through Plexiglas walkways, ramps take you up to the *Triceratops*' horns, skulls are there to be touched, knobs and buttons to be pushed and pushed again.

The most striking display is the main hall: an *Apatosaurus* rears up on its hind legs to protect her young from a rampaging *Allosaurus.* The creature's neck vertebrae, smaller and smaller, curl gracefully up to a tiny head just below the vaulted ceiling, as delicate and seemingly ephemeral as smoke.

The first time Helene suggested we take Dean there, I felt my heart jump just a bit. We went once, and then again. We'd range around the Hall of Saurischian Dinosaurs and the Hall of Ornithischian Dinosaurs, and then, Dean's dinosaurian obsession temporarily slaked, through the various halls of mammals, which are exactly as they were when I was little: buffalo roaming across the plains; antelope grazing near the Nile, a smoky brush fire in the distance; a gorilla pounding his chest in a misty rain forest, all safely behind glass, as well as dead.

The museum was never empty, and on rainy weekend days it was packed early, with bedraggled parents dragging platoons of soggy children from glistening SUVs with license plates from states near and far. On those days, the place was an exercise in frustration: the cafeteria packed with screaming, crying hordes, the crowds around the dinosaurs so thick that you could never get near the buttons or touch the skulls.

Now that Dean was hooked on something, I decided to take full advantage of it. What better person to answer this new deluge of questions than the top dinosaur guy at the American Museum, the curator of dinosaur paleontology? His name is Mark Norell. I set up an interview. I figured he could field Dean's queries while, at the same time, untangling some of mine. I wondered if his own childhood fascination with dinosaurs had brought him to this cathedral. Could Dean's interest propel him through a lifetime?

I took Dean out of school for half of the day. He'd be marked late, but I was confident that for this one morning at least he'd learn more with me than he would in his classroom.

We met Norell in his office on the top floor of the pointed turret of the museum's southeast corner. It's circular, with giant windows looking out on Central Park and the high-rises of the East Side of Manhattan, which were hazy and backlit by the morning sun.

"Do you live here?" Dean asked when we walked in.

"Sometimes I feel like I do," Norell said, getting up from behind his computer. He had longish, blond-gray hair, and looked a little like Steve Martin, the comedian. He was younger than I'd expected.

He gave us a tour, past rows of wooden storage cabinets, behind the scenes, to the various "bone rooms" where specimens are kept. We saw a bone from a *Camarasaurus*, a relative of *Diplodocus*, held in a frame of blond wood and thick Styrofoam, and some of Norell's recent finds from Mongolia: two fossils of *Oviraptorosaurs*, one still sitting on a nest of eggs, both of them still embedded in the crusty red rock-like sand of the Gobi desert.

As we did, we chatted, and Norell said some surprising things.

He had spent much of his career on microgenetics. His work in fossils had involved the study of mammals. "But when I was offered a job here," he said, "the only condition was, they said, 'If you come to work at the American Museum, will you work on dinosaurs?'"

The only *condition*? Had being here in this cathedral of dinosaurs redirected his passion to prehistoric reptiles? At least a little bit? After twenty years in newspapers, I knew that being exposed to a topic, again and again, can make you fascinated by it. Otherwise, you could go insane.

"No," he said bluntly. "I'm not really that interested in dinosaurs. I'm more interested in science, whether we can actually figure some of this stuff out, if we are clever enough to do that as opposed to just knowing a lot about dinosaurs."

He didn't stop there: "I'm not one of the people who sits around and thinks about dinosaurs, how they were and how they acted. To me they are data sets. They are pretty much identical to thinking about the DNA sequence of corn, of maize, which I did when I was working on regulatory genes. To me it's just about the questions."

Dean looked at him blankly. I guess I did, too. Corn? This field trip was not going as I had expected. The head of dinosaur paleontology at the American Museum of Natural History "not really that interested in dinosaurs"?

I asked him about the *Apatosaurus* and the *Allosaurus* in the entrance hall. Could she really have stood up on her hind legs like that?

"We can't say definitively yes or no," he said. "At the time we did it, it was judged to be sort of 'out there.' But less so, I think, now. There has been a lot of biomechanics work where people have actually been able to look at the range of motion, what was possible, and even though you can't test it directly, a lot of the people who work in biomechanics think that it was possible."

As he spoke, Norell opened sliding shelves containing every imaginable shape of fossil, hip bones, pelvises, vertebrae of every size.

"Is this early Cretaceous?" Dean asked about an *Ankeceratops* skull.

"No, late Cretaceous," Norell said dryly.

He left us after the second bone room. It was 10:00 on a Monday morning. I knew I was supposed to get Dean back to school, but I couldn't resist: here we were, in the cathedral of dinosaurs, all by ourselves.

We had the run of the place, unencumbered by crowds. The sunlight came down in slants from the big windows, and we moved in and out of the shafts. I stopped by a painting I remembered from my childhood—of flying dinosaurs high atop a cliff by the ocean at sunset—and Dean yelled to me from across the room. He was standing at the *Pachycephalosaurus* skull that you are allowed to touch, and that is usually mobbed. I nearly shushed him, but then realized that we were the only creatures within earshot who were not hundred-million-year-old fossils. I went over to him. It was the first time I got to touch that skull.

We made a circuit of the other high points, our voices echoing, our sneakers making little zippy sounds on the marble floors. We walked near the *Apatosaurus*, up on the see-through walkway, and compared a row of *Protoceratops* heads lined up in size order. We stopped in briefly at the prehistoric mammals and fish. Then it was time to go.

I got him to school just in time for recess.

The How and Why Wonder Book of Dinosaurs had bombed, but my father had better luck. One afternoon he dropped by with a used paperback copy of *The Dinosaur Heresies* by Robert T. Bakker, the latest in the long list of adult books he'd bought Dean that had begun a thousand years before with *Mack: Driven for a Century*.

This was a "chapter book," as Dean would say, dread in his voice, aerated here and there with drawings by the author. Dean loved the drawings, they were filled with energy, with jumping and striking meat eaters, teeth always bared, and their squealing, fighting prey. I read it to him in his room as he drifted off to sleep, the Styrofoam planets hung above our heads, lit like half-moons by the light next to the bed.

But then I did something I had never done before with one of his other bedtime books. After Dean's breaths became regular, his eyes covered by lids like full moons, I gave him a kiss, switched off the light and crept into the living room, *The Dinosaur Heresies* in hand.

I carried it with me to my green chair, turned on the light above me and kept right on reading.

The book came out in the late 1980s, and while I'm certain much about dinosaur scholarship has changed since then, to me it was all new, and it seemed to fill in the key blanks between the dumb, lumbering dinosaurs of my childhood and the fast and smart ones of Dean's. I'd been too intimidated by Norell, and surprised by his disinterest in dinosaur lifestyles, to ask him about the changes. But Bakker says it all right at the beginning: the long-accepted dinosaurian orthodoxy was terribly flawed, he realized one night while admiring the *Brontosaurus* skeleton at Yale's Peabody Museum—they didn't fail, done in by their weight and tiny brains, as had always been thought. No, they had succeeded spectacularly, dominating the earth for 130 million years. Humans, by comparison, have been around for only about half a million years.

Dinosaurs were the single greatest evolutionary success story in the history of the planet.

Bakker goes on from there, with the enthusiasm of a child. He fights the idea that mammals are the most adaptable, enduring creatures in existence—a theory created by mammals—by noting that there are far more species of reptiles, and far more species of reptile predators, in the world. He lists all the similarities dinosaurs share with birds. And he relishes every undeniably fascinating fact he relates, from the long muscle that stretched the whole way up *Triceratops*' frill that gave his jaw immense chomping power, to *Stegosaurus*' ability to flip his plates up or down depending on the angle of a predator's attack, to the duckbill's remarkable rows of teeth.

Bakker questions whether dinosaurs were actually cold-blooded, contradicting Darlene Geis, author of *The How and Why Wonder Book of Dinosaurs*, who wrote: "The climate was just right for them—warm and moist and comfortable for cold-blooded reptiles. Reptiles can be active only in warm climates."

Dean noticed me carrying the book as I walked him to school the next day. He was surprised when I told him I'd stayed up reading after he went to sleep, but quickly learned to take advantage of my nocturnal studies. He asked me what I'd learned.

"You know, duckbills, I know you don't like them, but they had these incredible teeth, rows and rows of them," I said as we crowded together beneath my umbrella. "Whenever one fell out, another would come in, forever. It's really amazing."

"I know," he said as we got to the end of the block. "They were the only dinosaurs who really chewed."

"Really? How do you know that?"

"One of my DVDs."

We got to school a minute later and I deposited him in his classroom. His coat went on the hook. Then I walked to the subway. I took the local, so I'd have more time to read.

"Is hummus like dinosaur poop?"

—DEAN, as I dipped a piece of pita bread in hummus

My answer:

"No. That's disgusting. Don't say that again."

Mark A. Norell, Ph.D., curator of dinosaur paleontology, American Museum of Natural History, New York City:

"Probably not. Fossilized excrement is called coprolite. We find a fair amount of it. The difficult thing is, say, which went with this animal or which went with that animal? By looking at it you can determine things like diets; for instance, there is some that has been attributed to *Tyrannosaurus rex* that has bone fragments in it. Other specimens have been attributed to plant-eating animals, and occasionally little pieces of plants you can still identify are present in it. Really, the only way to attribute coprolite with an animal is if you find a dead animal and you find a coprolite still impacted in it. That's extremely rare."

"Why do little kids love T-rex?"

—DEAN

Again, Mark A. Norell, Ph.D., curator of dinosaur paleontology, American Museum of Natural History, New York City:

> "Because it's the major marketing tool for all dinosaurs. It's what Godzilla was based on. It's what Barney was based on. Every old film that had dinosaurs in it would always have a T-rex. It's kind of a prototypical dinosaur."

Of course dinosaurs are only the beginning. Children love animals, extinct or extant, in their own house or behind a fence or a thick glass wall at the zoo. They project human qualities and emotions onto them—Are they mean? Do they cry? And they wonder about their strange traditions and habits like that other curious species in the house, the grown-up. After dinosaurs, big cats are a favorite of Dean's, tigers and lions and cheetahs, and perhaps most obsessively, ligers, which are a mix of lion and tiger and grow to incredible sizes. I brought him a tear sheet of a story in the *New York Post* about ligers, and he studied the accompanying photograph for days, even took it to school to show around. Then there are snakes and lizards and alligators and Komodo dragons, which Dean sees as sort of modern-day dinosaurs, although Robert T. Bakker might take issue with that.

"Are killer whales mean?"

—DEAN, at the aquarium

Martha Hiatt, supervisor of animal behavior and husbandry, New York Aquarium:

"Killer whales (*Orcinus orca*) are sometimes referred to as the 'wolves of the sea' based on their strategy of hunting in packs. This cooperation, combined with their speed (up to thirty miles per hour) and size (males can be thirty-two feet in length), make them superbly adept at hunting and capturing prey. Killer whales are the oceans' apex predators, which means they are at the top of the food chain. The function of an apex predator is to regulate populations by preying upon sick or weak animals.

"Humans qualify as apex predators as well, although most of us are quite removed from the process through which we acquire food. Still, whether we pull nets to catch fish or travel to the supermarket to buy fillets, we are relying on predatory behavior. Does that suggest humans are mean?

"Killer whales are highly social animals. The social structure is complex and is matriarchal, which means that the dominant animal is a female. An animal acquires dominance by displaying its fitness over others. Dominance displays and attacks in orcas, as in most toothed whales, frequently consist of chasing, biting, jaw popping, vocalizing and tail slapping. Like killer whales, humans are highly social with a sophisticated social structure. Perhaps we measure dominance by an individual's wealth, popularity or political office. Sometimes our pursuits are combative. Does that make humans mean?

"It might be said that 'mean' is in the eye of the beholder—be it for food or social position. It may not be pleasant for the subordinant, but it results in an individual's or group's survival."

"Do large animals need help to have sex?"

—DREW RICKARD, Burlington, Vermont (mother cannot recall his age when he asked)

Sue McDonnell, Ph.D., head of the equine behavioral program, Widener Hospital for Large Animals, Kennett Square, Pennsylvania:

"Usually not, but there are instances where individual couples, because they are a little mismatched size wise, may need some help. You maybe have a small horse, and you like her personality and her willingness to perform, but she is not quite big enough to jump the jumps. So you cross her with a large stallion, hoping to get a nice mix—a nice personality with some size. The mare may be a little too small for the stallion, so you may have to guide the stallion, for insertion. Of course, if they were out completely on their own they would use the terrain: the mare would stand downhill. Miracles can happen: a tiny little pony can breed a huge horse. Many stallions who have had active athletic careers have little aches and pains or disabilities that require some assistance from people. For example, there have been horses with weak hind legs who have had people support them from their hips so they don't fall off during mating.

"Another example is pigs. They've been bred to be so meaty that they are sometimes physically too chubby. So sometimes they need help. Pigs stay *in copula* for a very long time, like twenty to thirty minutes, before they consummate the act, and sometimes they are just too out of shape and too chubby to get the job done. So they need help to just sort of support them, or you can put the female downhill from the male a little bit so that gravity keeps them going in the right direction."

"Why do all animals have tails, except for us and chimpanzees and gorillas?"

—ISABELLA ROJAS BAUSO, age eleven, Portland, Oregon

Dr. Kristen Lukas, curator of conservation and science at Cleveland Metroparks Zoo:

"It is not just us and chimpanzees and gorillas that don't have tails. Other apes like orangutans, bonobos and gibbons do not have tails either. Animals such as the guinea pig or koala have very rudimentary tails, which means they are there even if you can't really see them. You have to think about what tails are for: they mostly provide balance for animals, particularly those that might live in trees, and for almost any animal that walks on four legs. A tail counterbalances the weight of the head at the front of the body. As humans became more upright and some apes started to brachiate—that's hand-over-hand locomotion—the need for a tail for balancing became less and less; so over time and through evolution it kind of faded out. One thing I should point out is that we do have the vestiges, or the remains, of a tail. Basically, the bottom three to four vertebrae of the human spine are fused together, and that's what's called your tailbone. That structure still anchors muscles like your butt muscle and it still really hurts if you fall on it. I know because I broke mine when I was a cheerleader in the eighth grade."

"How did the cat's tongue get rough?"

—GENEVIEVE BOUCHONVILLE, age four, Branchburg, New Jersey

Dr. Jill Mellen, education and science director, Disney's Animal Kingdom, Orlando, Florida:

"Cats' tongues are rough to help them eat. Cats are the ultimate carnivores and the ultimate predators: they capture prey bigger than they are, and they have these huge claws to bring their prey down, and then they eat whatever they've caught. And while they certainly use their teeth to pull off meat, where the tongue comes in is to get every last bit of meat off the bone. They have these great tongues and they have these little hook-like things, called papillae, on their tongues and they use them to scrape all the meat off the bones. Why did cats evolve to have these? Of course, no one knows for sure, but that has never stopped scientists from speculating. Cats eat meat and only meat, and if they are going to eat only meat, boy, they better get every little speck that's down there. This speaks to evolution. As the cat family evolved, it became more and more specialized, so, presumably, those cats that ate more meat, and fewer fruits and vegetables, were more likely to survive. If a cat can get a little more meat off the bone because it has a few more hooks on its tongue, then presumably it can survive longer and reproduce more successfully."

"If a poisonous snake bites another poisonous snake, will one of the snakes die?"

—CONNOR SULLIVAN, age nine, Fort Wayne, Indiana

John Kinkaid, animal care manager, Department of Herpetology, San Diego Zoo:

"If they are the same species—let's say a red diamondback rattlesnake bites a red diamondback rattlesnake—and no vital organs are punctured, then no, the snake that is bitten won't die—there seems to be some immunity. You might get a localized reaction, some swelling or something like that, but if they are the same species, the bitten snake will recover. But there are many venomous snakes that do eat other snakes, like king cobras."

"Does a sea horse know it's a sea horse?"

—DEVON CERMELE CINQUE, age four, Mountain Lakes, New Jersey

Jeff Mitchell, senior aquarist/diver, John G. Shedd Aquarium, Chicago:

"Well, our word for a sea horse is 'sea horse,' so whether or not the sea horse knows we call a sea horse a sea horse or we call it a beluga whale or whatever, a sea horse definitely knows when it sees another sea horse that it is the same animal as itself. The perfect example is that a male sea horse and a female sea horse are actually very monogamous during the breeding season. They may actually be monogamous for their whole life, we don't know. The male will stay in a small area about a meter square for the entire season—which can be up to nine months—and the female will be in an area over one hundred meters square, and the female will return to the same male every day, and they will actually do a little pair bonding dance, and they'll dance every day, and that dance can last anywhere from two minutes to five to ten minutes, and the day after he gives birth—because the male gets pregnant, not the female—the dance can last up to two to three hours before she deposits eggs into his pouch. He gives birth one day, and gets pregnant again the next day. They know that they know each other, that they are a pair, and that they are the same animal."

"Do elephants cry?"

—AVA EISNER, age five, Merrick, New York

Mike Keele, Deputy Director, Oregon Zoo, Portland:

"I don't believe anyone has proven that this is actually the case—I mean tears as a physical expression of an emotion. What we believe happens with not only elephants but with other animals is that they end up with a piece of sand in their eyes or something and because they don't have hands to clear it—although I guess elephants sometimes use their trunks—the best way to make it go away is for the eye to cleanse itself, and so tears drain down through the lacrimal duct, and if there's too much of it, it spills over and it appears as if there are tears on the face. When we talk about elephants and do they have emotions, I think for sure they do, because, for example, if a calf is removed from the herd, its mother reacts pretty violently—she'll trumpet, she roars, she is not happy, there is anxiety. The thing I think humans have a tough time with is that we are always looking for a way for an animal to express emotion that we are familiar with, such as crying, while they may have a completely different way of expressing emotion, something we've never imagined. But at least thinking that they do have emotions is a good thing; it gives them the benefit of the doubt."

"Do raccoons eat cats?"

—PETER ROY, age five, Montclair, New Jersey
(family owns two cats)

Dr. Brenda King, veterinary medical doctor, Montclair, New Jersey:

"No, not to the best of my knowledge. The only mammal that I am familiar with raccoons eating is an occasional mouse. I think one of the misconceptions some people have about raccoons is that they are aggressive animals, and I don't find them in general to be aggressive animals. In fact, I have a client who, for close to twenty years, had a whole family of raccoons living in back of his house, and they would share food bowls with his cats. There was a woman in Upper Montclair—for a while she had the same scenario going on on her side porch: she would put food out for some feral cats that lived nearby, and she would find the cats and raccoons dining together. The raccoons that I find to be more aggressive are the ones that have something wrong, like an illness; the rabid raccoon is going to be very aggressive. Any animal who is attacked or threatened is going to respond for its own protection; surely, if a dog should chase a raccoon, one would not be surprised to have the animal stand to protect itself. Yet when one thinks about raccoons' reaction to being chased by coonhounds, the raccoons tend to tree themselves versus standing their ground. Needless to say, if cornered, they would stand their ground."

"Can a crow peck your eyes out?"

—DEAN, on the way to school

Greg Butcher, director of bird conservation, National Audubon Society, Washington, D.C.:

"Yes it can. It would most likely happen if you picked one up or cornered it, and it was trying to defend itself. It would go for your head. It would be trying to peck you in the head to back you off. So if you put it in fear of its life, you should probably fear for yours.

"Most humans who interact with crows have brought them up since they were babies, and the crows feel like they are part of the family. They are very intelligent birds. They can be taught to do tricks. People find them very companionable. In fact, there really is this long history of human interaction with crows, both positive and negative. The negative is because black birds just don't have a good reputation. Crows look pretty formidable. They roost up in big flocks;

there is just some kind of ominous feeling about a sky full of crows flying to their roost."

"Why do lightning bugs light up?"

—MAXIMO GIOVANNI ROJAS BAUSO, age seven, Portland, Oregon

Carol Maier, entomologist and owner, Victoria Bug Zoo, Victoria, Canada:

"They light up as a form of communication for the purpose of mating. Both sexes light up. Usually the female is on the ground, or on foliage, and the males are flying around. The males start a specific code of lightning flashes, and the females recognize that code and flash in response. Once they've agreed that they are the same species and they want to mate, the males and the females will cue in to each other through this code. The males have really large eyes for finding these female flashes. Unlike most other insects, fireflies use visual cues instead of chemical.

"The flash itself is a complex chemical reaction. It is almost one hundred percent efficient—it creates very, very little heat, it's almost ninety-eight percent light. The chemical that lights up is luciferin, which requires an enzyme called luciferase. All species of fireflies have this chemical, some to a greater degree than others. There is a phenomenon we call the 'Firefly Femme Fatale.' This lightning bug will be lying on the ground, watching and responding to males of a different species for the sole purpose of attracting a male to her so she can eat him. So she gets a meal and she gets to accumulate his luciferin.

"The best lightning bug display that I ever saw was in a really remote location up the Sekonyer River in Borneo, in South Kalimantan, Indonesia. They were flying way up in the nipa palms. There were billions of them. It was like a fireworks display the entire night, like one big flashing Christmas tree explosion after another. It was really extraordinary."

10.

A Train to Sue

Dean had reawakened my interest in dinosaurs, and was teaching me about them. But now I discovered one of the great benefits of being a father and having a boy who wasn't quite so little anymore: if I could get him interested in the same things I was interested in, then I had a partner for whatever I wanted to do. He was a great excuse. I'm not big on sports, but the football- or baseball-crazed father knows this angle well: get your son into football or baseball and you've got it in the bag.

Suddenly, you are a boy again.

Dean's godfather had given him a paperback picture book called *A Dinosaur Named Sue* about a T-rex fossil at the Field Museum in Chicago. We read it at bedtime after we finished with Bakker, and became curious. Dean asked: "Why does that T-rex have a name like a little girl?" I knew why the boy in the Johnny Cash song had the same name—his father wanted to make him tough, a cruel joke—but didn't have any idea about this T-rex, one of the biggest and most complete such fossils ever found.

Rather than go online, or simply turn to the page that actually explained the mystery, I decided this was a great opportunity to find the answer by taking a trip. We would go to Chicago, just the two of us, just like my dad and I used to travel to Rochester, and we would find out for ourselves why this fierce carnivore had such a little-girl name.

And to get there, we'd take the train.

I have always loved train journeys, both those that I have experienced and those that have been described to me. Scenes from each stuck permanently in my memory, the images illuminated by the platform lights at strange hours of the day or night, the wheels shiny and greasy, the brakes hissing steam. My father remembers taking the Sunset Limited with his parents when he was ten, and standing beside a giant black locomotive in El Paso, Texas, just before sunrise. I remember, also in the predawn coolness, waiting to get aboard an Amtrak train on the way home from visiting my cousins in North Carolina at Christmastime when I was about the same age.

In high school, I did a loop around Europe with a bunch of friends, Eurorail tickets in our back pockets, taking as many overnight trips as we could to save on hotels. When Helene and I got married, our honeymoon included a night train trip, in this case the Paris-Amsterdam Express. I thought it would be very romantic, having sex on a train between two great European capitals, but that idea was banished from our heads when we discovered that our compartment wasn't private, and that we were sharing it with a Belgian businessman in silk paisley pajamas. He detrained in Brussels, but by then the moment had passed.

Two years later, we took the overnight express from Bangkok to Chiang Mai in Thailand, chasing cockroaches out of the compartment before switching off the lights and watching in the darkness as the brightly lit triangular roofs of temples, appearing magically levitated, glided by in the distance like low-flying airplanes. Then, a year before Dean was born, for a travel story, we set out on a three-day rail transit of Canada, with a layover in the Canadian Rockies two days in. Although Helene was a good sport, she was clearly weary of the rails by the time we reached Vancouver.

But now I had Dean.

Traveling with a child is a delicate art. They are not really designed to be good travelers, their attention spans and energy levels are not calibrated for long journeys, no matter how much they may be fascinated by the cars, planes or trains that carry them to their destinations. You can only look out the window of a plane or a car for so long. As a parent, your biggest worry is that your child's screeching and misbehaving will get on other travelers' nerves, just as screeching and misbehaving children got on your nerves when you were childless and traveling to Chiang Mai or across Canada and wondering, Why would anyone ever have one of those?

I'm not quite certain why I thought taking a five-year-old on an eighteen-hour train journey was a good idea; I figured we could range around the whole train if he got antsy, run up and down the corridors, go to the lounge. I would be giving us both the gift of a memory. I booked a compartment on the Lake Shore Limited for late June, with a return trip a day later after one night in a hotel.

The tickets were $800. As I read my credit card number to the Amtrak reservation agent, I realized that the gift of a memory was not cheap.

Dean was excited: the promise of a train journey to a faraway city, with meals at a rocking table and sleep in an upper bunk, the rails clicking rhythmically below, was pretty exotic. As the departure date drew near, he asked me repeatedly about what to expect: Would our compartment be bigger than the elevator in our building? Would there be a television? How many cars would the train have? What would we have to eat? What was the first thing, the absolutely first thing, we would do when we got to Chicago?

We had lunch with Helene in the neighborhood on the big day—Brenda was watching Paulina—and then took the subway into the city, my bag filled with our clothes, Dean's backpack heavy with games and puzzles and books, his growing hand in mine. Since we had booked a sleeper, we got to use Amtrak's lounge in Penn Station, which included complimentary beverages. Dean loved this concept, and we spent most of our lounge time at the soda machine. Then the Lake Shore Limited was announced. We went down to the platform and then all the way to the end, to sleeperland.

The compartment was smaller than the elevator in our building: just two seats facing each other next to a big window and a small shelf to the side that flipped up to reveal a toilet (each compartment had one). Everything was stainless steel and had a very solid feel. The compartment had a small television screen above one of the seats, but our porter, Jay, said it didn't work; he wasn't sure if it ever had.

We unpacked the games and a CD player (for which I'd burned a disk of Dean's favorite songs), then stowed our bags and took our seats facing each other. The train started to move in that smooth, unannounced, almost imperceptible way trains do, and soon we were out of the darkness and shooting up the Hudson. We passed stone walls scarred with graffiti, and shore-front parks where couples posed for wedding photographs, and the spans of bridges with names like Tappan Zee, Mid-Hudson, Kingston-Rhinecliff and Rip Van Winkle.

I tried to teach Dean chess but we both grew quickly frustrated. He looked through a picture book and got his famous paper cut. He listened to his CD for three minutes. I was about two pages into the book I was reading about the Battle of Leyte Gulf when he took off the headphones and said he wanted to tour the train.

We headed through the two sleeper cars, palms against the sides of the corridors to keep steady, until we got to the lounge car. Jay had told us it would be closed until Albany, but I figured we could go through and see what was on the other side. Dean pushed the square button that opened the door with a hiss, and we walked in. The attendant was behind the counter, his back to us, counting inventory.

"You can't come in here," he said, not turning around. "We're closed."

"We just want to go through."

"I said we're closed. You can't go through." Now he turned.

"But . . ."

"I said we're closed."

I felt myself getting very angry. I'd paid $800 for this trip, and I'd be goddamned if I was going to be spoken to that way in front of my son.

Here's a memory from my childhood:

I went through a lengthy samurai movie phase beginning when I was twelve. My dad and I went to a double feature of Japanese films, *The Loyal 47 Ronin*, parts one and two. But we got there late—only single seats remained. Two were in the front row, with a man sitting between them. Slouched down and balding, he was staring straight ahead with his hands in a triangle in front of him, fingertips to fingertips, thumb tip to thumb tip. I walked up to him and politely—and I've been told I was an unusually polite kid—asked if he would mind moving over one seat so my dad and I could sit next to each other.

He looked at me, and at my father, and back to the white screen and said, "Yes, I would mind. I'd mind twice. Once for you, and once for him."

I was surprised but didn't really care; my dad and I would just sit one seat apart.

But my father radiated rage.

He stepped forward and said, "Stand back, Wen, while I kick this man's face in."

It was a hugely uncharacteristic threat of violence from my dad, and although the man in the seat between two empty seats didn't even look up, I was horrified by the thought of a fight and pulled on my father's sleeve until he backed down. We sat on steps in the aisle for both films, neither of which I remember, except that they were very long and that the climactic sword fight took place off-screen. But I can still recall the feeling of abject terror in my stomach, my pulse racing, at the thought of my dad rolling in the aisles, kicking and punching some artsy arthouse movie guy from 1978 who wouldn't move over one seat.

Now I was standing in the café car of a Chicago-bound train, my legs still unused to the rocking sensation, and Dean was looking at me just like I must have looked at my father nearly thirty years before. I didn't want him to feel that same feeling of terror, and I could see from his eyes that it was coming on. Nor did I want his chief memory of this trip being that of me, his father, cursing and spitting as I hurled myself over the snack counter to wrestle with the lounge attendant.

He tugged on my sleeve. I gave Mr. We're Closed the dirtiest dirty look I could muster and we went back out through the hissing door.

By dinnertime, the Hudson was smaller. We ate in the dining car with an older woman and her granddaughter, who was six, a year older than Dean. The woman lived outside Schenectady and was taking the little girl for the weekend so her son and his wife could have a break. They'd been late getting to the station in Albany, where they boarded, but luckily her son knew someone who worked in the control room, and the train had been held.

I asked her what was news in her part of the world, and she became very animated and went into some detail about a virulent strain of algae that had clogged all the rivers and streams near her house. Dean followed along, energized by her enthusiasm.

"Is it, like, really disgusting?" he asked.

"Oh, I've never touched it," she said.

Then she added: "How much fun it must be for you, taking an overnight train with your dad."

When we got back to our compartment it was made up for sleeping; Dean was unconscious after less than two minutes of back scratching. I got comfortable in my bunk, sipping a little flask of bourbon I'd brought along, reading about Leyte Gulf. This didn't last long; soon I was asleep, too, waking only when the train made a station stop. I'd roll over and brush the curtain aside to see where we were and some yellowy light would filter in. Once, I saw our dinner companions walking to a waiting car, its blinkers on; later I saw the 1:00 a.m. skyline of Rochester, and I thought sleepily of the trip my dad and I had taken here when I was about Dean's age.

When Dean and I woke up, Lake Erie was out the corridor window, framed like a moving diorama. It was a bright sunny day. "It's not a lake, it's an ocean: you can't see the other side," he said as we went to breakfast.

We ate with a British couple who had traveled from Swindon in the south of England to London, via train, then flown to New York, and were now training it to Chicago and then Milwaukee to see Tom Petty & the Heartbreakers.

Dean was impressed. "You took a train and a plane and a train again to hear music?"

"We sure did, mate."

"Do a lot of people do that?"

"Don't know, really."

The four of us hit it off. They were surprised that I knew that the band XTC came from Swindon; I was surprised that the woman had been involved in an ill-fated Web venture with Dave Gregory, XTC's guitarist. Swindon must be a small town, I thought. (Actually, according to 2002 statistics, the population is 153,700.)

Dean and I went back to our compartment after breakfast to pack up for Chicago. But trouble rode the rails. I had noticed during the night and during breakfast that the train stopped a lot for no apparent reason. When we were still outside Gary, Indiana, the flaming tops of its oil refinery smokestacks off in the distance, I realized we were going to be late; we'd already been aboard for eighteen hours. I silently cursed our algae-obsessed dinner companion for making the train wait in Albany. I worried about the Swindon rockers' Milwaukee connection.

And I worried about Dean.

He had been busy and interested throughout the trip, but he reverted to the five-year-old he undeniably was when we pulled onto a siding yet again to let a freight train rush by. I pointed out the flaming smokestacks. I suggested he count the cars of the passing train. Neither interested him. He began to sob.

"Why does this train always stop?" He pounded his fist on the table. "Why doesn't the television work?"

Now the compartment seemed much, much smaller than the elevator in our building.

We got into Chicago at noon, four tear-filled hours later.

But then we saw her.

The Field Museum's main dinosaur exhibit was closed for restoration, but a traveling show of fossils from China had just opened; it included specimens Mark Norell had brought back to the United States. As we went through it, I was reminded yet again about how much dinosaurs had changed since I was a child: these new varieties were more outlandish and unpronounceable than any we'd previously encountered: *Mamenchisaurus, Caudipteryx, Toujiangosaurus, Monolophosaurus.*

That's a bloody mouthful, as our breakfast companions might have said.

Dean could pronounce every one, putting to rest my final worries about his speech. But these Chinese beasts, as impressive as they were, were only a warm-up. The T-rex named Sue stood by herself on the first floor, visible in the distance over the heads of those lining up for tickets.

Standing in the museum's soaring main hall, Sue was different from any fossilized skeleton we'd seen before. She did not appear to be static, standing upright and lording it over those around her, but was instead crouched over, her haunches up, like she was in the midst of a final sprint to catch her quarry. The T-rex at the American Museum of Natural History is crouching, too, but Sue's movements had an almost liquid-like fluidity to them; you could practically see the flexing muscles in her massive thighs, and those little two-fingered forearms quivering excitedly as her teeth plunged into some foolish duckbill's back, and that whipping, surprisingly elegant tail in motion.

I knew that Sue was nearly an entire skeleton; the one in New York was a mixture of two. A painting of Sue in happier times—that is to say, when she had flesh and muscle and a functioning brain—hung beneath the hall's ceiling, above a frieze supported by Ionic columns, showing her hunting beneath a purply late-Cretaceous sunset.

Dean's eyes went wider than usual as he nodded his head in silent acknowledgment of the beast. Then he bent forward, double talons out, and started working on his own impersonation of this exciting new stance.

I read to him about Sue. She was discovered in South Dakota in 1990. This made me smile: she was still buried when I became obsessed with dinosaurs in first grade and would be for fifteen more years, until the year I started dating Helene, who would eventually give birth to the little boy standing—or bending and roaring, all three feet, ten inches of him—next to me.

She was the sightseeing high point of our trip. Everything that followed, including German U-boat 505 at the Museum of Science and Industry, which we checked out the next day before getting on the train for New York, was somehow diminished by her malevolent greatness.

But she was not the most important discovery of the trip for me. Back in my little lower bunk, Dean asleep above me, my flask nearly empty and the Japanese at Leyte Gulf nearly vanquished, I thought about the last three days. More specifically, I thought about Dean and realized that my pride in my son had welled up in a way it never had before as we sat with our companions at dinner and breakfast.

He talked so easily and inquisitively. I had seen it begin with Ron Charles—"*Daddy—remember that time. The bumper?*"—and Mark Norell—"*Is that early Cretaceous?*" But now he was a full member of the conversation—"*Is it, like, really disgusting?*" "*You took a train and a plane and a train again to hear music?*"

When he asked the last one, I felt like cheering. The little girl with whom we'd had dinner, cute as she was, hadn't said a word.

Once Dean had been a baby, and then a toddler, cute and funny, but now more than ever he was a real person. My feelings toward him, toward the person he had become, were evolving. He asked me questions, I answered or I looked for answers—but sometimes now I asked, too. His discovery of dinosaurs had been a revelation to me: he had let me see the world through the eyes of a child, and reminded me of mysteries and wonders I'd forgotten. Somehow, being on a trip, traveling, just one on one, father and son, made these changes dramatically clear to me. This was what I learned.

I put down my book and switched off the reading lamp. The compartment was dark except for the occasional light flying by, its reflection flashing across the stainless steel. The tracks clicked fast beneath us; the Lake Shore Limited was making good time.

"Why does that T-rex have a name like a little girl?"

—DEAN

William F. Simpson, collections manager of fossil vertebrae, Field Museum of Natural History, Chicago:

"It's named after the woman who discovered it, and her name was Sue Hendrickson. She was part of a commercial paleontology company that was searching for and digging up dinosaurs in western South Dakota. The head of this company named the dinosaur after her because it was such a stunning discovery—the largest, most complete T-rex ever found. But even though we call it Sue, we really have no idea what gender this particular *Tyrannosaurus* was—it might be a boy named Sue. As sort of an aside, when I was growing up, dinosaurs didn't have names like this. They had their scientific names and that was it. Sue was one of the first, and started a trend of the big rock stars of the dinosaur world getting their own names. I even named my own dinosaur here at the Field Museum. It is a juvenile *Tyrannosaur*, and it was found by our first curator of vertebrae paleontology, Elmer Riggs. So in the new tradition of always naming a dinosaur after the discoverer, the specimen is now known informally as Elmer."

"Is there such a thing as a nice dinosaur?"

—MINA PAZ-LE DRAOULEC, age three, Hastings-on-Hudson, New York

Again, William F. Simpson, collections manager of fossil vertebrae, Field Museum of Natural History, Chicago:

"It depends on what nice means. There were dinosaurs that ate other animals, and I think that they would probably not be viewed as nice, since they were predators. But there were hundreds and hundreds of plant-eating dinosaurs, and unless you were a plant, I think you could view them as nicer. Some of them were gigantic, so you'd have to be careful if you were alive and around them; even if they didn't want to eat you, they could still hurt you by accident. But another way of answering that is that there is no nice or not nice in nature: that is a human construct. I don't think that we know of any animals that kill for fun, other than human beings. Certainly human beings alone in nature understand the ramification of killing something, which makes it meaner of us to kill than it would be otherwise."

"Why does this train always stop?"

—DEAN, just outside Gary, Indiana, when he should have been arriving in Chicago

Bill Crosbie, Senior Vice President of Operations, Amtrak:

"There are three primary reasons. First, what we call 'freight-train interference'—other trains on the line. We travel at a higher speed than they do—typically seventy-nine miles per hour, and they typically travel at fifty to sixty miles per hour—so we would overtake them. It really comes down to congestion. Then, in the interest of safety, there are various wayside detectors for dangers like hot wheels and hot bearings. It's a voice warning that tells the engineer to stop the train immediately. Usually, the conductor or the assistant conductor will go out and do an inspection on the train. The next reason, the last reason, would be the owner of the railroad, the company that owns the right-of-way. We rely on the freight railway network outside of the Northeast Corridor; when you take a trip like on the Lake Shore, you are traveling as a guest on that railway, and we have an operating agreement with them. Railways try to keep their right-of-way—their tracks, the bridges, their signals—in a state of good repair. And they do that in the daylight hours. In the interest of safety, workers put a block on the section of track where they are working, and they have to clear that before allowing the train to go through. Sometimes the tracks, the rails, are removed, and you'd have to wait on that until they get them back in place."

"Why doesn't the television work?"

—DEAN, trying to kill time outside Gary, Indiana

Again, Bill Crosbie, Senior Vice President of Operations, Amtrak:

"We've made the decision here to discontinue the televisions in the sleeper cars. It was unbelievably expensive to maintain them, and that's due to the working environment. It is a standard television built for your living room—it is not built for being shaken around on a train trip. It was very frustrating for our customers. We debated internally on both sides whether to replace them. There were arguments on both sides whether to keep them or take them out; because of the maintenance, we decided to take them out. They are all disconnected, but I guess some screens still haven't been removed."

"Is it, like, really disgusting?"

—DEAN, asking about a bloom of ravenous algae in upstate New York

Rob Moore, Executive Director of Environmental Advocates of New York:

"There are several types of different algae; some can form slimy or disgusting mats of green stuff and some do not. Some can even pose a health risk, like blue-green algae, which can secrete a poisonous substance. Algae are something that are always present in freshwater bodies and are actually the base of the food chain, serving as food for small fish that are in turn eaten by bigger fish. So algae are actually a very important part of a water body's ecology. When you start getting too many nutrients that algae feed upon—like nitrogen and phosphorus—you throw the water body's balance out of whack, and the result are large blooms of algae that can form thick mats of slimy stuff that looks like vegetation. It depends on what type of algae you have. If you were dealing with filamentous algae, for example, you may have this mat floating on the water, and it's oozy and slimy, gross; it kind of sticks to things, it gets on the side of your boat. Other types of algae may just form little clumps that make the water appear very cloudy."

"Do a lot of people do that?"

—DEAN, learning that an English couple had traveled from Swindon, England, to London to Chicago to Milwaukee to see Tom Petty

Miriam Plastow, high school attendance secretary living just north of Toronto, Canada, and a devoted Tom Petty fan:

"Tom Petty & the Heartbreakers fans who live outside of the United States have no option but to travel a long way if they want to see their favorite band live in concert. The band no longer tours outside of the country. The last time they performed in Toronto was in 1999. This year I will be driving to Saratoga, New York, to see a show, then I'll be flying to Philadelphia the following week to see another one in Camden, New Jersey. The farthest I've gone so far to see this band was several years ago, when I flew out to

California from Toronto to catch two shows. I've also seen the band in Chicago and New York. I know of one fan who has flown several times from England to the United States for this, and this year one of the fans is flying all the way from Australia to Arizona to see a show. Tom Petty is always saying how lucky he is to have such a lot of loyal fans. Well, we're either loyal or have more money than sense. By the way, I have been extremely fortunate enough to meet Tom Petty & the Heartbreakers backstage before a show in New York at Madison Square Garden on December 13, 2002. It was one of the most exciting experiences of my life."

"Can you get struck by lightning on Metro-North?"

—NICK MANSKE, age seven, Brooklyn, New York, after reminding his mother that trains, unlike cars, do not have rubber tires

Robert Walker, former head of the power department, Metro-North Railroad:

"If you are sitting on a train, then, no, you cannot get hit by lightning. You are shielded by the body of the car, which is made of metal and is grounded by the metal wheels riding along the steel rails. A Metro-North car, or a Long Island Rail Road car, or any other passenger train car is basically a metallic shield that is protecting you from the lightning above. Could one of the cars get hit by lightning? Yes—there would be a large bang, people inside could hear it, but nothing would happen to the people; the charge would just travel through the metal and go down to the earth. We have had lightning hits on the railroad, particularly on the New Haven Line, where we have overhead catenary lines. But as long as you are inside the car, with all the metal around you, it is much safer in a lightning storm than being on a golf course or being under a tree. That's the glory of it. Now, if you were on a Metro-North platform, the odds go up that you could get hit. But I don't remember ever hearing of anybody getting hit on a platform."

"Why does the plane swing out over the ocean?"

—SAM ROSEN, age eight, Montclair, New Jersey

Captain Arnold Reiner, Delta Airlines pilot (retired), and former director of flight safety, Pan Am:

"Planes normally take off and land into the wind, because they get better performance that way. So if you are coming into Los Angeles from New York and the winds are from the east, you will swing out over the Pacific Ocean in order to get lined up to land toward the east. But not every time: if the winds are out of the west, you will come in straight from the continent. When you leave from New York, because the airports are in the vicinity of water, you will frequently go out over the water; very often air traffic controllers will try to do that to minimize the noise over populated areas. When you take off from John F. Kennedy Airport on Runway 31 Left, which is the preferred runway for international departures because it's the longest, you'll turn to the left as quickly as you can to avoid overflying the city, and end up heading south over the ocean. It's a less noisy route to city residents and the flight track avoids the city's tall buildings. And it's a safer route. If an engine failed early in the departure, there would be less thrust to climb and you would want to ascend in a less obstructed area, which would be over the water."

"In Antarctica, are people upside down?"

—JORDAN MAINZER, age eight, Highland Park, Illinois

Liesl Schernthanner, winter manager, South Pole Station, Antarctica:

"When standing here at the bottom of the Earth, I don't feel upside down. My feet are on the ground and the sky is above me, so I'm perfectly right-side up. An astronaut in outer space may look at me and notice that my head is pointing in the opposite direction as someone standing at the North Pole; from the same view, someone in New York may look somewhat sideways. Thanks to gravity, we're all grounded on the Earth with our heads towards the clouds, and we're all right-side up relative to our location. Life is all about perspectives."

"Why did the Egyptians build pyramids? Why not giant rectangles or some other shape?"

—ALEKS SIEMASZKO, age eleven, Montclair, New Jersey

Dieter Arnold, curator of the Department of Egyptian Art, The Metropolitan Museum of Art, New York City:

"Egyptologists assume that they represent primeval hills, the hills that on the day of creation rose out of the flood. This idea certainly comes from the natural state of Egypt in former times. Egypt was flooded by the Nile, and when the flood retreated, islands appeared and they are considered to be symbols of re-creation, of the day of creation. So a pyramid could represent such a hill. But one could ask: Why was it not just a rounded hill, why did it have edges leading to a top? Another idea has to do with the rays of the sun, because sometimes one can see the rays of the sun in Egypt falling in a pyramid shape on the desert surface. So a pyramid could also be a place where a king climbs up to his heaven. But these are all speculations. Do you want a third theory? In the Egyptian city of Heliopolis—this was the center of the sun cult in Egypt—there was a monument called a benben stone. This was apparently a kind of sacred stone. It's gone now. It could be that this benben stone had the shape of a pyramid, and that the people who built the pyramids were trying to re-create that, because the top piece of a pyramid is called a benben."

"Why don't they make mummies anymore?"

—JAY RUSSELL, age five, Brooklyn, New York

Dr. Gunther von Hagens, Heidelberg, Germany, anatomist and inventor of Plastination, a method for preserving dead bodies:

"Every culture of old preserved bodies by natural methods to avoid decomposition. The most developed method of preservation was mummification practiced by the Egyptians; eventually it became very elaborate. First, the brain was removed through the nose with the aid of a hook. This idea was both disgusting and fascinating to me when I was young. I imagined it was maybe like noodles. The body was then slit open and everything except the heart was removed, washed in palm oil and preserved in a jar in alcohol. The body was washed and filled with powdered myrrh, resins and perfumes and the slit was sewn back together, and then placed in a preservative solution for seventy days. Then it was washed, rubbed with oils or resins and wrapped in many layers of linen bandages. Despite all this work, only the skin and bones were permanently preserved.

"Mummies are no longer made for religious reasons, but technology, science and a human desire to become immortal has opened the door for new preservation methods. Human nature is still drawn to mummification as a means of ensuring immortality. A modern method of mummification is Plastination, a process that I invented in 1977 at the University of Heidelberg in Germany, in which all bodily fluids and soluble fats are removed from the body and replaced with polymers like silicone. Plastination preserves so well that it reveals the beauty beneath our skin frozen in time between death and decay. It is available to anyone who is interested in having his or her human remains preserved for health education of future generations. A poll of Germans showed that ten percent would consider Plastination as an alternative to conventional burial. After thousands of years, modern mummification is regaining interest in modern society."

Epilogue

The Dinosaur Heresies was only the first of many dinosaur books I read. But I never told Dean everything I learned about that dinosaur called Sue.

I didn't tell him how Sue Hendrickson found the T-rex embedded in a cliff in South Dakota while on a dig with Peter Larson, a private fossil collector who had been her boyfriend, or that in the months and years following the find the discovery turned into an international controversy. The federal government seized Sue the dinosaur, saying it was the property of the rancher on whose land it was discovered, even though he had accepted a check from Larson for $5,000. Prosecutors eventually charged Larson with currency violations and illegally digging for fossils on private and federal lands.

I didn't tell Dean how Hendrickson had to testify against Larson at his trial, after being barred from speaking to him for three years, and that Larson spent nearly two years in prison after being convicted of felony currency violations and two other misdemeanors. Or that Sue the dinosaur, after languishing in a storage facility for years while the legal dramas played themselves out, was eventually auctioned to the Field Museum with financial backing from McDonald's and Disney.

She sold for $7.6 million.

Why tell Dean all this? Why spoil the mystery and romance of that graceful crouching skeleton waiting at the end of our overnight train journey with the details of lawsuits, and arcane federal land regulations, and hostile witnesses, and newspaper headlines, and jail time, and big corporate dollars?

Sometimes, what he doesn't know won't hurt him.

And when I think about Sue and what Dean doesn't know about her, I wonder, really, what do we know about anything?

We know that volcanic ash shuts down jet engines and policemen eat doughnuts because they are easy to replace and that getting stabbed feels like getting punched. We know that tickling is an attack and elephants don't cry and that there is a reason they put the rope on the left side of your neck when they hang you. We know there are 25,393,690 lights in New York City and that the Beatles grew up and that fire doesn't travel from brownstone to brownstone. We know that doctors write illegibly because they are impatient and sea horses dance because they've been reunited and pigs sometimes need help to have sex because they are fat, and we know that cats and raccoons have been known to dine together. We know that John Dean was always very solicitous of his wife, Maureen. And we know that billions of lightning bugs swarm like exploding Christmas trees in the nipa palms above the Sekonyer River in Borneo.

But there's a lot we don't know.

We're not entirely certain why the dollar sign has an S in it—maybe it was the pesos, maybe not. We don't know if those dancing sea horses are monogamous their entire lives, but we are trying to find out. We don't know who first said "spoon." We don't know what would happen if a jetliner hit the Empire State Building or why the Egyptians made the pyramids in the shape of pyramids, but we have theories, tons of theories, and people whose job it is to speculate about such things and make very educated guesses. And we don't know if that *Apatosaurus* in the American Museum of Natural History, rearing up on her hind legs to protect her young from an *Allosaurus*, really did that, though we'd like to think so, and the biomechanics experts think it was very possible.

I hope the day never comes when someone proves she couldn't, whether because her legs were too weak, or her neck too long, or her torso too heavy. Whatever the reason, it would be a disappointment.

Facts can intrude on your imagination, can rob you of the wonderment that comes with being a child.

I really appreciate Geoffrey Patterson, Oscar-nominated sound mixer, explaining why the highway is so noisy, putting to rest in a minute of explanation a lifetime of confusion. It is actually quite interesting that some municipalities and states use old tires in their asphalt to bring down the noise. Or that reducing noise by ten decibels is actually perceived by the human ear as reducing it by half. That's something I never would have guessed had he not told me—I doubt the question would even have occurred to me.

But imagine just for a minute if he was wrong. Think of the brilliance, the magnificence—not to mention the cacophony—if all the homeowners in all the towns up and down the Long Island Expressway, from Great Neck to Riverhead and everywhere in between, in all those split-level ranches on all those cul-de-sacs, had switched on their vacuum cleaners via a prearranged signal at the exact moment the Jamieson family in its blue Volkswagen went bouncing by.

Now *that* would really have been something.

Dean and all the other children who asked questions reminded me, at forty, not to take the world at face value. Why do we use the words we use?

"Why is it called kidnapping if you can steal away adults, too?"

I figured finding the answer would be easy: I'd just call the FBI and whoever answered the phone would be able to explain why that word is used even though children aren't the only ones you can grab off the street. But one official passed me to another. It took a lot of research. For the detective, for the prosecutor, for the kidnapper, even for the kidnap victim languishing in a storage locker like Sue, without food or water and wondering if his family will pony up the cash, the word is just taken for granted.

Until a child hears it.

Dean saw a picture of a volcano erupting beneath a towering upside-down mountain of ash and smoke. And he asked: *"What happens if your plane flies over a volcano?"*

It was the first thing that entered his mind, and it seems obvious enough. But Captain Eric Moody and his crew had no idea what was happening when they flew on that dark old night into the plume of ash from Mount Galunggung and their engines shut down one by one. They kept it cool in the cockpit, but for fourteen long minutes they were certain they were dead. No one, until then, had truly understood what happened. Now airplane manuals come with warnings. The language is very stiff and official but the meaning is clear: "Whatever you do, DO NOT fly your jet into a plume of volcanic ash."

Jacob Sklodowski was four when he saw the *Mona Lisa* in an Elmo Halloween movie, and again in store displays. How many adults have gazed at this painting and tried to unlock the secret of that faint quarter-smile? How many others have stood on line at the Louvre in Paris and then been surprised by just how small and seemingly inconsequential it is?

But Jacob looked beyond the canvas, off the edge—literally, out of the box. What is happening in the world we can't see, he asked, and what, just what, is she wearing on her feet?

"Does Mona Lisa wear shoes?"

I was disappointed when Mark Norell said he wasn't that interested in dinosaurs. But now I think maybe he had a point when he said, "I'm more interested in whether we can actually figure some of this stuff out, if we are clever enough to do that, as opposed to just knowing a lot about dinosaurs."

Because sometimes the questions are better than the answers. And sometimes, no matter how good the answers are, they can be swept away.

Think of my grandfather, Pop Pop. I had used his age—ninety-five—and relative good health to explain to Dean that he need not fear his death or mine anytime soon. Pop Pop was born when horses still pulled wagons down the street, I told him. Lots of time passes in a single lifetime. But then Pop Pop threw my analogy into disarray. He died.

His last few months had been rough ones, in declining health in a nursing home, and the last time we saw him he looked like a grayish wax facsimile of my grandfather, just vaguely familiar, asleep with his mouth open when we walked into the room. I wasn't sure he knew we were there. But after he woke up and we all talked at him for a while, he looked at me and said, "You're wearing new pants!" in his familiar deep voice. And I was, and I laughed. When we left, Dean gave him a long hug.

He died a month later, and I worried how this would affect Dean. But he was more fascinated than upset; dying is interesting, no doubt about it. We drove back to Pennsylvania for the memorial service. There was a big dinner party the night before, and my cousins from North Carolina were there, and maybe a hundred other people, and Dean and Paulina charmed them all, running around on the giant lawn behind the house, trying to catch the first lightning bugs of the evening.

Then there was Pluto.

It still hangs in Dean's room. I'm sure the top half is covered with dust—I haven't been up there lately. But it's not the planet it used to be.

The battle in the astronomical community about what Pluto should be called raged long after that night four years ago when Helene and I hung those Styrofoam balls—or I hung them and she advised me. We had decided to just let it remain a planet, not a plutino, as some observatories and planetariums had reclassified it. But the wails of protest from around the world eventually became too much for us to ignore.

In the summer of 2006, scientists gathered for a meeting of the International Astronomical Union. They traveled from around the world and convened in Prague, and after much debate, finally, and once and for all, threw Pluto out of the planets. To have the honor of being a planet, they agreed, one must orbit the sun, one must be spherical and one must have cleared its orbit of all other objects. Pluto failed this last one, cutting as it does across the icy detritus of the Kuiper Belt.

But their final decision was more than just a banishment. It was a humiliation.

Pluto, they decided, was not a plutino, or a small planet or a block of ice.

Pluto was a "dwarf planet."

And so a debate was ended once and for all, and the answer determined—at least until the next meeting, in Paris or Chicago, next year or next decade, when a new theory is put forward and a new vote is taken and Pluto is invited back into the elite brotherhood of round, sun-orbiting, orbit-clearing celestial bodies.

When that happens, we'll be ready with our little Styrofoam ball.

I'll never forget my dad explaining Watergate. He took so much time to lay it all out for me, unaware, I suppose, that he'd gone sailing over my head after the first sentence. But I appreciate what he was doing, and have tried to do the same for Dean: treat him like an adult, take him seriously, even when he's asking if the hummus I'm about to eat is like dinosaur poop. In a funny way, when my father made up an answer, he was taking me seriously, too; he was making a joke he figured I'd get. And eventually, I did.

I understand this phenomenon better now: the urge to invent can sometimes be very strong, especially when finding the answer takes longer than you think it will, or when people you are certain have the answers won't call you back or are evasive and confused when they do.

But kids these days are not like kids in my kid days. They are hard to fool, even harder to impress and nearly impossible to scare. The entire world is cynical and disbelieving, and they start picking up these traits early. If you want to shock their imaginations, well, you've really got to pour it on.

Last summer I was driving Helene and the kids back to our little cottage in the country. We passed a Dunkin' Donuts in a strip mall. Dean, like many children, harbors a strange fascination with this and all fast-food chains. I had been in there buying coffee and doughnuts the previous Monday, at 6:00 a.m., going in the other direction, on my way to work.

Dean and Paulina seemed to be occupied in the backseat. I started talking to Helene.

"Boy, if you want to see something scary, stop in at that Dunkin' Donuts at six a.m. on a Monday. There were these two tiny women there, each with giant hair. They were in front of me. One got six sugars in her coffee, one got eight. And they were smoking these long cigarettes."

"Eight sugars?" Helene said, suitably impressed.

But the word "scary" had traveled over our headrests and punched its way into my son's consciousness.

"Wait," Dean said from the backseat, suddenly paying attention. "What happened?"

"Oh, nothing. I was just telling Mommy about the last time I was in this Dunkin' Donuts."

"You said it was scary."

"Yeah, a little bit."

"What was so scary?"

"These women with big hair. They wanted a scary amount of sugar in their coffees."

"That's not scary."

I thought for a moment. Helene rolled her eyes. I looked in the rearview mirror to see Dean's expression. It was a bored expression. I decided to fix that.

"And there was this man there in a Dracula suit; he was covered in blood."

"That's not scary."

"And there was another man—well, he wasn't a man, he was half-horse, half-wolverine, and he was running around terrifying everybody."

"Really?"

"Yeah. And then this half-horse, half-wolverine tore off this kid's leg and went galloping down Route 58 with the leg in his mouth, and the kid's mother went running after them, screaming, '*That half-horse, half-wolverine has my kid's leg! That half-horse, half-wolverine has my kid's leg!*' And people were crashing through windows, falling on the glass, shrieking and yelling and getting scalded with hot coffee. Then the police came and they were shooting everywhere and I got hit in the shoulder. Twice."

"Really?"

"Yeah, really."

"That is scary."

"Damn straight it was scary."

My father would be proud.

That afternoon I took Dean and Paulina for a walk so they could see what I did for fun back in the days before million-channel cable systems and video games. I had bought an Estes toy rocket and a couple of engines and a launcher that morning, and I thought they might get a kick out of seeing what I did on my ninth birthday, when my dad took me and my friends up to the park.

Dean and his sister trundled along the gravel road in the woods. I walked behind them with the equipment for our space shot. They get along pretty well, these two, although Dean does enjoy torturing her and making her scream, and she has developed a surprisingly strong right hook for a three-year-old. When Paulina first came home from the hospital, her arrival didn't seem to bother him: she was more pet than person; by the time she started to cut into his time with his parents she was already part of the scenery and there didn't seem to be any jealousy. Still, he has asked me some questions that suggest trouble: a few nights earlier, hungry at dinnertime, he eyed her while she had a tantrum, and asked why we couldn't just cook her.

Now I looked at her walking ahead of me, her pink-and-white sneakers crunching the gravel, her light brown hair catching the errant streaks of sunlight that snuck through the trees. She was coming into focus in my mind as Dean did during his post-truck, early-dinosaur days.

I wondered what questions she will ask me. Will she be as curious about physical injury, falling buildings, carnivorous beasts and crashing planes as her brother is? Will she tell my secrets to the used-car salesman? Will "Why?" become her mantra, repeated like a mystical chant? Or will she find her own methods of interrogation? She has already taken to the girl path as Dean took the boy path, without, really, any encouragement from us—she likes ballet as Dean likes play-fighting, dolls as Dean liked trucks and buses. She picks her own outfits and wants everything to match; Dean wouldn't care if we sent him to school wearing a garbage bag. Helene was a tomboy when she was a girl and has no idea how this happened. We've given up, for now, trying to figure it out.

Will she ask me one of those great, moment-stopping questions that have, at the same time, no answers and a hundred answers, the kind that make you stop and think: Where did that come from? What is going on in this child's brain? And how come I never thought of that? I'm sure she will. Those questions are my true joys; they speak to a world where anything is possible, where nothing cannot be explained and nothing can be explained, a world where we never grow up.

We came into the field and set up in dry grass that stung our bare legs; I'm sure it was filled with ticks and poison ivy. We avoided the droppings from the deer we'd seen at night jumping through our high beams. I slid the rocket onto the launcher and inserted the igniter into the engine as if it had been only minutes, and not thirty-one years, since the last time I'd done it. I unspooled the wire, crouch-walking backward, and sat down cross-legged in the grass with my son and daughter.

"How far will it go?" Dean asked.

I told him I couldn't answer that: we didn't know the weight of the rocket, the thrust of the engine, the current wind velocity or the angle of our shot. I didn't tell him that even if I knew those things, I still would have no idea how far our rocket would fly.

We had a countdown, and he pushed the button and the little rocket shot up over the field with a *phffffffffffffffffffffffffft*, trailed by white smoke. At its apex—I wondered if you could see the Dunkin' Donuts from up there—the parachute popped out and it started falling down to Earth, swinging back and forth, smelling of sulfur even at a distance. Dean went running for it.

I don't think I could have been any happier than I was sitting in that field in the waning late August sun. I wouldn't have minded if everything in the world had just stopped while that little rocket hung up there. The sky was as clear as it had been on my ninth birthday, but it was later in the day, later in the season, and it was a darker blue, almost violet—the wavelengths of the sun's light scattered across the heavens. Gnats flitted around our heads as Paulina and I watched Dean get smaller and smaller. The rocket fell farther than I'd expected; his tiny shape looked out of breath as he bent down to pick it up. Well, at least he had his answer.

Then I felt a disturbance in the universe. It was just a hint, as hard to detect as the first half-inch of a long-distance train trip, but it was unmistakable. I looked off to the bushes and trees at the edge of the field, but quickly realized the disturbance was emanating from somewhere closer, much closer, and a bit lower. It was coming from the tiny girl in my lap. I looked down. She stared up at me.

She said, "Where's the deer?"

I looked at her.

"Oh, I don't know," I said. "Sleeping, I guess."

She stared at me some more. I stared back at her. I felt the need to fill in the silence.

"They're, you know, nocturnal. They sleep during the day and go out at night."

She crinkled her eyes, eyes as big as her brother's when he asked his first question. Her gaze hardened. And then she asked:

"How come?"

Dear Dr. Taylor:

I am a New York author seeking to interview someone who is familiar with animal species or primitive cultures that engage in cannibalism. It would be a quick interview, and could be done on the telephone, or via e-mail. It is for a book I am writing in which I seek experts to answer the questions of children. The question I need answered is one my son, Dean, asked about his little sister, Paulina, while she was having a tantrum during dinnertime.

He asked: "Why can't we just cook her?"

I'd like a serious answer: why cannibalism is not socially accepted, if it ever was, and if it once was in some cultures, why it is nonetheless unlikely that one would have cooked and then eaten one's little sister. Or perhaps it was common. I don't know. She certainly looks tasty.

Sincerely,

Wendell Jamieson

"Why can't we just cook her?"

—DEAN, pointing at his sister

Timothy Taylor, M.A., Ph.D., FSA, reader in archaeology, Department of Archaeological Sciences, University of Bradford, United Kingdom:

"You cannot just cook and eat your sister, because your father is trying to civilize you. You would find it existentially upsetting. Even if you were uncivilized, like the seventy-plus species of mammal who are known cannibals, it would not be your sibling you would kill and eat. For instance, male lions and female chimpanzees kill and eat the offspring of rivals, not infants who are closely related to them genetically. In a cave I was excavating recently, I discovered the ancient remains of butchered babies and toddlers, so I know that early humans certainly sometimes ate other humans. It was not always their enemies. Before farming was developed to provide regular meals, if a member of your family died, it would have made nutritional sense not to waste anything, and you would not want to attract dangerous meat-eating animals to your camp or allow your enemies a chance of a good feed off your deceased loved one. So in those circumstances you would have been obliged to eat your little sister, as part of a solemn, dutiful ritual. Nowadays you don't need to do that, unless times get very, very tough. So keep your fingers crossed that civilization continues—our sort, that is. The apparently civilized Aztecs deliberately terrorized, sacrificed and ate bits of their own children. Their priests were obsessed with being scary, and were not—in my opinion—nice people."

"Does Mona Lisa wear shoes?"

—JACOB SKLODOWSKI, age four, Wilmington, Delaware, after seeing a mock *Mona Lisa* in an Elmo Halloween movie, and then in store displays for *The Da Vinci Code*

Douglas W. Strong, medieval-footwear researcher, author of numerous booklets and DVDs on how to make medieval footwear, and a historical reenactor who is a longtime member of the Society for Creative Anachronism:

"Certainly she is wearing shoes. The year of the painting—1503 or 1504, we don't know exactly—is on the cusp of shoe-making technology between medieval shoes and more modern shoes. I think with the *Mona Lisa* we would be looking at medieval shoemaking because you find this style a little later in Italy than you do in northern and northwest Europe. Also, this older style persisted as indoor shoes even as the newer style became available. And since she is sitting for a portrait, she would be indoors. Even though the background is outdoors, she probably wasn't sitting in a field.

"The newer style was not all that different from a good pair of modern dress shoes: when you look down you can see the sole sticking over the top of the shoe; the sole attaches to a thinner layer of leather that is attached to the shoe. The older style of shoe is called a 'turn shoe'—a shoe that is sewn inside out and then turned as part of its construction. So you didn't see the seam, and the sole didn't extend beyond the bottom of the shoe, if you looked at it downward. She was probably wearing a turn shoe that would look like a house slipper today—a low, slip-on shoe, with no fastening at all. It would have a short, fairly blunt point, a little like a gothic arch. No heel, nothing extra added on. Color is tough to determine because most of the shoes that survive from that time are all dark brown and black—by this point, they've been in the ground a long time. But it is not unreasonable to think she has brown shoes on."

"What would it be like if whatever we were supposed to be doing, we didn't really do?"

—KATIE EPSTEIN, age five, Brooklyn, New York

She is asked to elaborate on this by her mother.

"I mean, if when we were supposed to go to lunch we went to lunch, but instead of eating we just sat and stared at each other? And if we went to school, but instead of learning we all just sat and stared at the teacher, and she stared back? What if we went to my ballet recital next month, and all got dressed up in our tutus, and then just stood there and stared at the audience, and they stared back, and when it was all over the audience clapped and we curtsied and left?"

HER MOTHER: "Wow, Katie. That . . . would be really weird!"

David Miller, secretary, Existentialist Society, Melbourne, Australia:

"It would be a far simpler matter if we were being asked, 'What if there was no communication?' Or even the more drastic 'What if there was no action?' However, in two of these scenarios, the Performance and the Lesson, although there is no verbal communication, there is, in the Performance, a type of nonverbal communication in the form of 'clapping.' Also, in the two scenarios there is much 'staring' at each other by both sides. Is this communication? It could be argued that—yes it is. On the other hand, staring could be seen as a form of contemplation, and not necessarily communication.

"There is certainly loads of activity implied in both scenarios—getting out of bed, getting dressed and having breakfast, for starters. Assembling in the auditorium in one scene, and in the classroom in the other. The staring. The leaving of the auditorium and the classroom. Going home, etc., etc.

"The question is almost, 'What if we stopped everything in the middle?' If we stopped in the middle, then others might also stop what they are doing in the middle. We rely on others completing what they have commenced. If they stopped in the middle, it could be disastrous. Imagine. Planes would fall from the sky. Soup would burn on the stove. Financial markets would fail. Cities would be plunged into darkness. So we all take on the mutual obligation to complete what we have started. It is called cooperation.

"All my musings have so muddied the waters and befuddled my brain that I no longer know what it is that I'm being asked."

"What else?"

—CAMPBELL ROBERTSON, aged four to eleven, Montevallo, Alabama, whenever relatives would bring him gifts

Bhante H. Kondanna, abbot, Staten Island Buddhist Vihara:

"Many experience the feeling of never having enough. We often do not view this as a negative experience, as in the case of not having enough money, love, clothes or myriad other possessions. We never seem to be satisfied; we always need more to enable us to reach that elusive point of total satisfaction.

"We must be mindful that if this desire for more becomes an obsession, then it will be a hindrance rather than a helper. If we are obsessed with our desire for more, whether it be for material things or even spiritual ones, we may lose sight of our true goal in the process. Sometimes, we can be so caught up in seeing what we don't have, that we don't see what we do have. Remember that we always have enough if we are but willing to accept what is. Possibly there is only one apple in the fruit basket, and some part of us may feel that one is not enough. Yet with a higher perspective, we can see that one apple is all we need at the moment, that one is enough and that when we require more, more will indeed be available.

"Because the unwholesome tendencies spring from seeds buried deep in the bottom-most strata of the mind, to eradicate these sources of affliction and nurture the growth of the liberating vision of reality, the Buddha presents his teaching in the form of a gradual training. It does not burst into completeness at a stroke, but like a tree or any other living organism, it unfolds organically. If we follow through the comparison of the Buddhist discipline to a tree, virtue would be the roots, for it is virtue that gives grounding to our spiritual endeavors just as the roots give grounding to a tree. Hence for a proper spiritual life to flourish, the foundation must be laid in childhood. It is essential at the outset to nourish the proper roots, otherwise the result will be frustration, disillusionment and perhaps even danger.

"Lord Buddha says in the Dhammapada:

Epilogue

When a person lives carelessly and unmindfully,
his desire grows like a creeping vine.
He runs now here; and now there,
as if looking for fruit: a monkey in the forest.

If this sticky, unrefined desire
overcomes you in the world,
your sorrows grow like wild grass
after rain.

If, in the world, you overcome
this unrefined desire, hard to escape,
sorrows roll off you,
like water beads off a lotus.

Notes on Sources

Questions not from Dean came from the children of friends, acquaintances, colleagues and strangers, who submitted them to www.fatherknowslessbook.com. Some children who asked have since grown up. Answers were collected on the telephone, via e-mail or in person; some were edited for grammar, length and continuity, always with the answerer's full knowledge. Beyond that, answers are the words of those who participated, as are any opinions expressed. The answers from Mark H. Anders, Peter Bogdanovich, Richard Burke, Salvatore J. Cassano, Dr. Sudhir Diwan, Martha Hiatt, James Lipton, Mark A. Norell, Dr. Anna Nowak-Wegrzyn and Iris Weinshall appeared in my story in *The New York Times* on January 26, 2006.

In the essays, some names have been changed to protect the potentially embarrassed. Dinosaur information came from *The Dinosaur Heresies* by Robert T. Bakker (William Morrow and Company, 1986); *Tyrannosaurus Sue: The Extraordinary Saga of the Largest, Most Fought Over T-Rex Ever Found* by Steve Fiffer (W. H. Freeman and Company, 2000); and *Encyclopedia of Dinosaurs* (Parragon, 2002). Information about Pluto, and its diminished status, came from Dennis Overbye's fine reporting in the *Times.* Information about Estes rockets was provided by the Estes Company. All other sources are noted in the text.

Acknowledgments

All books are collaborations, but this one is more than most. Thank you first to all the parents who remembered their children's questions and shared them, to all the children who asked them and to everyone who answered, from Yoko Ono to John Timoney to Liesl Schernthanner at the bottom of the world. Thank you to my agent, Jay Mandel, who worked the phones, and to my editor, Dan Conaway, who answered the call even though I stood him up for lunch. Thank you to Dr. Sudhir Diwan, Gianine Rosenblum, Peter Bogdanovich and Mark A. Norell for taking the time to explain, and to Anthony Petrosino, Mike Virk, Lauren Rubin and William Crawford, who read and advised. Thank you to all the reporters at *The New York Times* who helped me find answer people, especially Fernanda Santos, who interviewed Carlinhos de Jesus, samba dancer and choreographer, and translated his words from the Portuguese; and to my colleagues, past and present, on the Metropolitan Desk, especially Anne Cronin, who was so enthusiastic about the original story; Susan Edgerley, who is so enthusiastic about everything; Kyle Massey, who wrote the headline; and Joe Sexton, my friend and mentor, who gave me my dream job. Thank you to my parents, Bessie Jamieson and Walter Jamieson, Jr., who always listened and always did their best; to my stepparents, Kathy Jamieson, Tom Boyle and Robert M. Kulicke, who helped fill in the blanks, and to my sister, Lindsay Gallagher, my co-witness to history. And to my mother-in-law, Irene Stapinski, who makes the forties sound like so much fun.

Finally, thank you to my daughter, Paulina, who taught me to type with one hand, and to my son, Dean, whose truly singular view of the world changed mine. And most of all, to my wife, Helene, who has done so much to give the little ones great beginnings, childhoods of wonder and excitement, and who taught me that if you write what you really want, and you write the truth, only good will come of it.

About the Author

Wendell Jamieson is city editor of *The New York Times.* He grew up in Brooklyn and lives there still, with his wife, Helene Stapinski, and their children, Dean and Paulina.